Collins

Teacher's Guide 3
Spelling Skills

Author: Sarah Snashall

HarperCollins
P U B L I S H E R S
—200—

William Collins' dream of knowledge for all began with the publication of his first book in 1819.

A self-educated mill worker, he not only enriched millions of lives, but also founded a flourishing publishing house. Today, staying true to this spirit, Collins books are packed with inspiration, innovation and practical expertise. They place you at the centre of a world of possibility and give you exactly what you need to explore it.

Collins. Freedom to teach.

Published by Collins
An imprint of HarperCollins*Publishers*
The News Building
1 London Bridge Street
London
SE1 9GF

Browse the complete Collins catalogue at
www.collins.co.uk

© HarperCollins*Publishers* Limited 2017

10 9 8 7 6 5 4 3 2 1

978-0-00-822310-6

All rights reserved. No part of this publication may be reproduced, stored in a retrieval system, or transmitted in any form by any means, electronic, mechanical, photocopying, recording or otherwise, without the prior written permission of the Publisher or a licence permitting restricted copying in the United Kingdom issues by the Copyright Licensing Agency Ltd., 90 Tottenham Court Road, London W1T 4LP.

British Library Cataloguing in Publication Data

A catalogue record for this publication is available from the British Library.

Publishing Director: Lee Newman
Publishing Manager: Helen Doran
Senior Editor: Hannah Dove
Project Manager: Emily Hooton
Author: Sarah Snashall
Development Editor: Jessica Marshall
Copy-editor: Tanya Solomons
Proofreader: Gaynor Spry
Cover design and artwork: Amparo Barrera and Ken Vail Graphic Design
Internal design concept: Amparo Barrera
Typesetter: Jouve India Private Ltd
Illustrations: Alberto Saichann (Beehive Illustration)
Production Controller: Rachel Weaver

Printed and bound by CPI Group (UK) Ltd, Croydon, CR0 4YY

Contents

MILTON   HOUSE
LEEK ROAD
MILTON
STOKE-ON-TRENT
ST2 7AF
TEL: 01782/234780
E-MAIL: milton@milton.primary.org.uk

About Treasure House

Treasure House is a comprehensive and flexible bank of books and online resources for teaching the English curriculum. The Treasure House series offers two different pathways: one covering each English strand discretely (Skills Focus Pathway) and one integrating texts and the strands to create a programme of study (Integrated English Pathway). This Teacher's Guide is part of the Skills Focus Pathway.

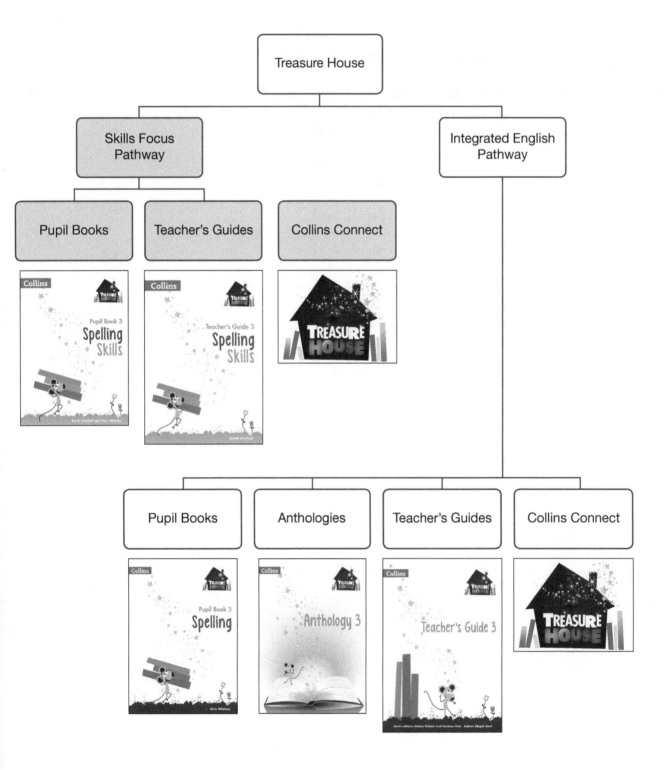

1. Skills Focus

The Skills Focus Pupil Books and Teacher's Guides for all four strands (Comprehension; Spelling; Composition; and Vocabulary, Grammar and Punctuation) allow you to teach each curriculum area in a targeted way. Each unit in the Pupil Book is mapped directly to the statutory requirements of the National Curriculum. Each Teacher's Guide provides step-by-step instructions to guide you through the Pupil Book activities and digital Collins Connect resources for each competency. With a clear focus on skills and clearly-listed curriculum objectives you can select the appropriate resources to support your lessons.

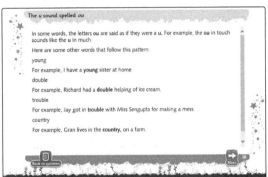

2. Integrated English

Alternatively, the Integrated English pathway offers a complete programme of genre-based teaching sequences. There is one Teacher's Guide and one Anthology for each year group. Each Teacher's Guide provides 15 teaching sequences focused on different genres of text such as fairy tales, letters and newspaper articles. The Anthologies contain the classic texts, fiction, non-fiction and poetry required for each sequence. Each sequence also weaves together all four dimensions of the National Curriculum for English – Comprehension; Spelling; Composition; and Vocabulary, Grammar and Punctuation – into a complete English programme. The Pupil Books and Collins Connect provide targeted explanation of key points and practice activities organised by strand. This programme provides 30 weeks of teaching inspiration.

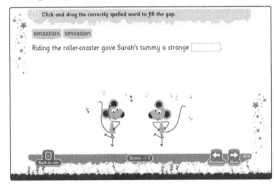

Other components

Handwriting Books, Handwriting Workbooks, Word Books and the online digital resources on Collins Connect are suitable for use with both pathways.

Treasure House Skills Focus Teacher's Guides

Year	Comprehension	Composition	Vocabulary, Grammar and Punctuation	Spelling
1	978-0-00-822290-1	978-0-00-822302-1	978-0-00-822296-3	978-0-00-822308-3
2	978-0-00-822291-8	978-0-00-822303-8	978-0-00-822297-0	978-0-00-822309-0
3	978-0-00-822292-5	978-0-00-822304-5	978-0-00-822298-7	978-0-00-822310-6
4	978-0-00-822293-2	978-0-00-822305-2	978-0-00-822299-4	978-0-00-822311-3
5	978-0-00-822294-9	978-0-00-822306-9	978-0-00-822300-7	978-0-00-822312-0
6	978-0-00-822295-6	978-0-00-822307-6	978-0-00-822301-4	978-0-00-822313-7

Inside the Skills Focus Teacher's Guides

The teaching notes in each unit of the Teacher's Guide provide you with subject information or background, a range of whole class and differentiated activities including photocopiable resource sheets and links to the Pupil Book and the online Collins Connect activities.

Each **Overview** provides clear objectives for each lesson tied into the new curriculum, links to the other relevant components and a list of any additional resources required.

Teaching overview introduces each spelling rule and provides a list of key words that follow the rule that are useful to the age group.

Support, embed & challenge supports a mastery approach with activities provided at three levels.

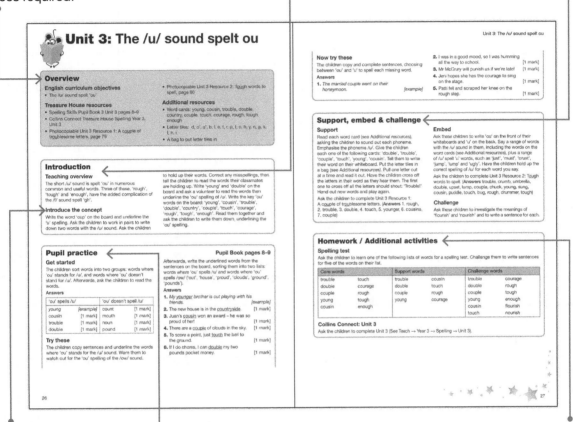

Introduce the concept provides 5–10 minutes of preliminary discussion points or class/group activities to get the pupils engaged in the lesson focus and set out any essential prior learning.

Pupil practice gives guidance and the answers to each of the three sections in the Pupil Book: *Get started*, *Try these* and *Now try these*.

Homework / Additional activities lists ideas for classroom or homework activities, and relevant activities from Collins Connect.

Two photocopiable **resource** worksheets per unit provide extra practice of the specific lesson concept. They are designed to be used with the activities in support, embed or challenge sections.

Treasure House Skills Focus Pupil Books

There are four Skills Focus Pupil Books for each year group, based on the four dimensions of the National Curriculum for English: Comprehension; Spelling; Composition; and Vocabulary, Grammar and Punctuation. The Pupil Books provide a child-friendly introduction to each subject and a range of initial activities for independent pupil-led learning. A Review unit for each term assesses pupils' progress.

Year	Comprehension	Composition	Vocabulary, Grammar and Punctuation	Spelling
1	978-0-00-823634-2	978-0-00-823646-5	978-0-00-823640-3	978-0-00-823652-6
2	978-0-00-823635-9	978-0-00-823647-2	978-0-00-823641-0	978-0-00-823653-3
3	978-0-00-823636-6	978-0-00-823648-9	978-0-00-823642-7	978-0-00-823654-0
4	978-0-00-823637-3	978-0-00-823649-6	978-0-00-823643-4	978-0-00-823655-7
5	978-0-00-823638-0	978-0-00-823650-2	978-0-00-823644-1	978-0-00-823656-4
6	978-0-00-823639-7	978-0-00-823651-9	978-0-00-823645-8	978-0-00-823657-1

Inside the Skills Focus Pupil Books

Comprehension

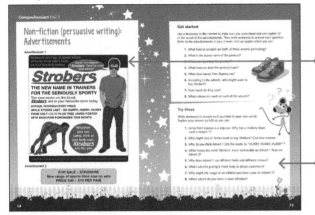

Includes high-quality text extracts covering poetry, prose, traditional tales, playscripts and non-fiction.

Pupils retrieve and record information, learn to draw inferences from texts and increase their familiarity with a wide range of literary genres.

Composition

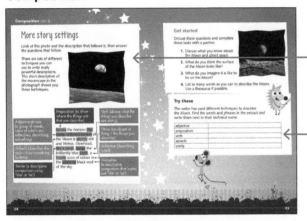

Includes high-quality, annotated text extracts as models for different types of writing.

Children learn how to write effectively and for a purpose.

Vocabulary, Grammar and Punctuation

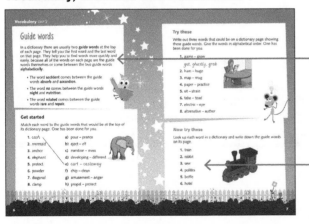

Develops children's knowledge and understanding of grammar and punctuation skills.

A rule is introduced and explained. Children are given lots of opportunities to practise using it.

Spelling

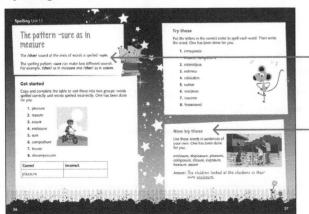

Spelling rules are introduced and explained.

Practice is provided for spotting and using the spelling rules, correcting misspelt words and using the words in context.

Treasure House on Collins Connect

Digital resources for Treasure House are available on Collins Connect which provides a wealth of interactive activities. Treasure House is organised into six core areas on Collins Connect:

- Comprehension
- Spelling
- Composition
- Vocabulary, Grammar and Punctuation
- The Reading Attic
- Teacher's Guides and Anthologies.

For most units in the Skills Focus Pupil Books, there is an accompanying Collins Connect unit focused on the same teaching objective. These fun, independent activities can be used for initial pupil-led learning, or for further practice using a different learning environment. Either way, with Collins Connect, you have a wealth of questions to help children embed their learning.

Treasure House on Collins Connect is available via subscription at connect.collins.co.uk

Features of Treasure House on Collins Connect

The digital resources enhance children's comprehension, spelling, composition, and vocabulary, grammar, punctuation skills through providing:

- a bank of varied and engaging interactive activities so children can practise their skills independently
- audio support to help children access the texts and activities
- auto-mark functionality so children receive instant feedback and have the opportunity to repeat tasks.

Teachers benefit from useful resources and time-saving tools including:

- teacher-facing materials such as audio and explanations for front-of-class teaching or pupil-led learning
- lesson starter videos for some Composition units
- downloadable teaching notes for all online activities
- downloadable teaching notes for Skills Focus and Integrated English pathways
- the option to assign homework activities to your classes
- class records to monitor progress.

Comprehension

- Includes high-quality text extracts covering poetry, prose, traditional tales, playscripts and non-fiction.
- Audio function supports children to access the text and the activities

Composition

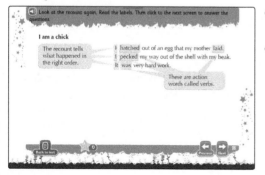

- Activities support children to develop and build more sophisticated sentence structures.
- Every unit ends with a longer piece of writing that can be submitted to the teacher for marking.

Vocabulary, Grammar and Punctuation

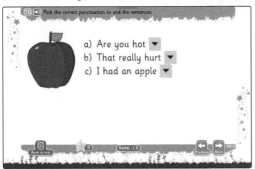

- Fun, practical activities develop children's knowledge and understanding of grammar and punctuation skills.
- Each skill is reinforced with a huge, varied bank of practice questions.

Spelling

- Fun, practical activities develop children's knowledge and understanding of each spelling rule.
- Each rule is reinforced with a huge, varied bank of practice questions.
- Children spell words using an audio prompt, write their own sentences and practise spelling using Look Say Cover Write Check.

Reading Attic

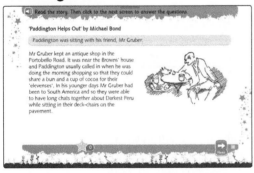

- Children's love of reading is nurtured with texts from exciting children's authors including Micheal Bond, David Walliams and Micheal Morpurgo.
- Lesson sequences accompany the texts, with drama opportunities and creative strategies for engaging children with key themes, characters and plots.
- Whole-book projects encourage reading for pleasure.

Treasure House Digital Teacher's Guides and Anthologies

The teaching sequences and anthology texts for each year group are included as a flexible bank of resources.

The teaching notes for each skill strand and year group are also included on Collins Connect.

Support, embed and challenge

Treasure House provides comprehensive, detailed differentiation at three levels to ensure that all children are able to access achievement. It is important that children master the basic skills before they go further in their learning. Children may make progress towards the standard at different speeds, with some not reaching it until the very end of the year.

In the Teacher's Guide, Support, Embed and Challenge sections allow teachers to keep the whole class focussed with no child left behind. Two photocopiable resources per unit offer additional material linked to the Support, Embed or Challenge sections.

Support

The Support section in Spelling offers scaffolded activities (suitable for use in small groups with adult support) that will help learners who have not yet grasped the specific spelling rule. These activities use fewer or more straightforward words and are usually supported with a photocopiable resource sheet.

If you have a teaching assistant, you may wish to ask him or her to help children work through these activities. You might then ask children who have completed these activities to progress to other more challenging tasks found in the Embed or Challenge sections – or you may decide more practice of the basics is required. Collins Connect can provide further activities.

Embed

The Embed section includes activities to embed learning and is aimed at those who children who are working at the expected standard. It ensures that learners have understood key teaching objectives for the age-group. These activities could be used by the whole class or groups, and most are appropriate for both teacher-led and independent work.

In Spelling, the Embed section provides activities to embed learning following the whole class introduction and is aimed at those who children who are working at the expected standard. After the children have learnt each rule, this section provides a range of fun small group games and activities to help the children (working without an adult) to learn words with the spelling pattern. A photocopiable resource sheet is provided for each unit.

Challenge

The Challenge section provides additional tasks, questions or activities that will push children who have mastered the spelling rule without difficulty. This keeps children motivated and allows them to gain a greater depth of understanding. You may wish to give these activities to fast finishers to work through independently.

Children who are working above the expected level may progress to focusing on the spelling of less common, longer words or they might investigate exceptions to the rule and creating posters for the class. Challenge activities are provided to stretch the children's understanding of the rule or to enhance vocabulary work.

Differentiated spelling lists

In the Homework section, you will find word lists for spelling tests. There is a standard list and there are also two targeted lists; *Support words* list is suitable for children who are struggling with the concept. The list is shorter and contains words that are more common, shorter, simpler or more regular. The *Challenge words* list is a longer list often with more challenging words, suitable for children who have grasped the rule/concept.

Differentiated weekly spelling lists are provided for each unit and details of any matching Collins Connect units.

Assessment

Teacher's Guide

There are opportunities for assessment throughout the Treasure House series. The teaching notes in the Skills Focus Teacher's Guides offer ideas for questions, informal assessment and spelling tests.

Pupil Book Review units

Each Pupil Book has three Review units designed as a quick formative assessment tool for the end of each term. Questions assess the work that has been covered over the previous units. These review units will provide you with an informal way of measuring your pupils' progress. You may wish to use these as Assessment *for* Learning to help you and your pupils to understand where they are in their learning journey.

The Review units in the Spelling and Vocabulary, Grammar and Punctuation Pupil Books, include questions testing rules taught in preceding units. By mixing questions on different unit topics within exercises, children can show understanding of multiple rules and patterns.

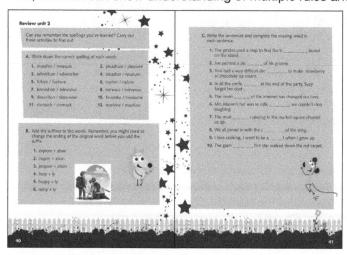

Assessment in Collins Connect

Activities on Collins Connect can also be used for effective assessment. Activities with auto-marking mean that if children answer incorrectly, they can make another attempt helping them to analyse their own work for mistakes. Homework activities can also be assigned to classes through Collins Connect. At the end of activities, children can select a smiley face to indicate how they found the task giving you useful feedback on any gaps in knowledge.

Class records on Collins Connect allow you to get an overview of children's progress with several features. You can choose to view records by unit, pupil or strand. By viewing detailed scores, you can view pupils' scores question by question in a clear table-format to help you establish areas where there might be particular strengths and weaknesses both class-wide and for individuals.

If you wish, you can also set mastery judgements (mastery achieved and exceeded, mastery achieved, mastery not yet achieved) to help see where your children need more help.

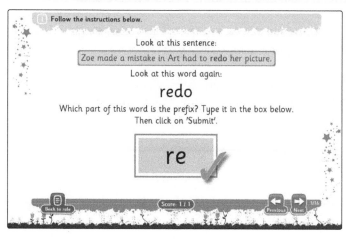

Support with teaching spelling

Trying to teach and understand the vagaries of English spelling is enough to drive the most patient of us to distraction. Think on those lucky countries such as Poland with phonetically consistent spelling. However, many words in English are phonetic and this should remain our starting point for all unknown words, with the children becoming increasingly confident in their knowledge of the spelling options for each sound.

The National Curriculum in England encourages us to teach the rules and patterns that are associated with each spelling cluster. In some cases these rules are easy to absorb, for example 'i before c except after c'. Others remain more elusive, such as hearing the stress in a word before deciding whether to double the last letter or not. You will have to judge for yourself when the rule is going to aid children in their learning and when they would be better off just learning the rules. (There are times when you have just got your head around a complicated rule to discover that there are only five suitable words for your class.) However, a knowledge and understanding of rules that do apply will provide children with the skills to manipulate language and root words, such as by adding suffixes and prefixes, to create specific vocabulary for their writing. This in turn will increase their confidence in writing. Teaching children to understand the relationship between words, such as 'grace' and 'gracious' not only develops their vocabulary but aids their spelling too.

This spelling scheme by its nature focuses on learning words as a separate activity: games, spelling tests and sometimes sentences. But, of course, this is only part of the picture. Children who read a lot will naturally absorb spelling as they regularly come across common words. Children who write a lot will naturally practise words that they want to use. Learning to spell words is only of any use if you use them at some point. Therefore, the activities in this scheme can only form part of the picture.

Weekly spelling test

The weekly spelling test remains crucial to learning the huge bank of words needed by the end of primary school. Spelling lists are provided in this scheme, but you may want to add or remove words depending on the abilities of the children in your class and the number of words you feel it is appropriate for them to learn. You will need to strike a balance between developing their vocabulary and providing useful words for them to learn.

You may also wish to enhance their spelling lists with words that they have spelt wrong during their writing tasks, or specific topic-led vocabulary.

Spelling games

The activities in this scheme aim to be fun and game-like. Many of the activities in the book are introduced for use with a particular set of words but many can be adapted for any word list you are practising (they mainly involve creating a set of word cards):

Pairs: Create two sets of word cards for the words you are practising and use them to play a game of pairs. Alternatively, use words with and without suffixes and prefixes or words related in other ways (such as different spellings for the same sound or homophones) and challenge the children to find the two associated words.

Simon's Game: When asking the children to learn a specific set of words, such as words with 'c' for /s/, ask pairs of children to remember the words on the list.

Pick a card: the children place a set of word cards between them and take turns to draw a card and test their partner or the next child around the table.

Hangman: Tell the children to play Hangman using words from previous two or three weeks' spellings. This encourages an attention to the specific letters and can be particularly useful when practising words with silent letters.

Bingo: Create Bingo cards for the words you are studying (ensuring each card has a slightly different word selection). When playing Bingo, the children spend the session staring at the words on their sheet – a useful way to add the word to the subconscious.

Game board: Create a simple board game where the children roll a dice to progress along a series of squares some of which require them to spell one of the words from the list (when someone draws a card and reads it to them). The board can be reused with any new set of words cards.

Differentiation

The lesson plans in this book provide three levels of differentiation. However, you may wish to provide further practice (Support or Challenge) at Years 3 and 4 or Years 5 and 6 by supplying the relevant children with the book for the other year group, as the words covered are the same. You may also wish to recap on words from earlier years for those children whose spelling needs further help.

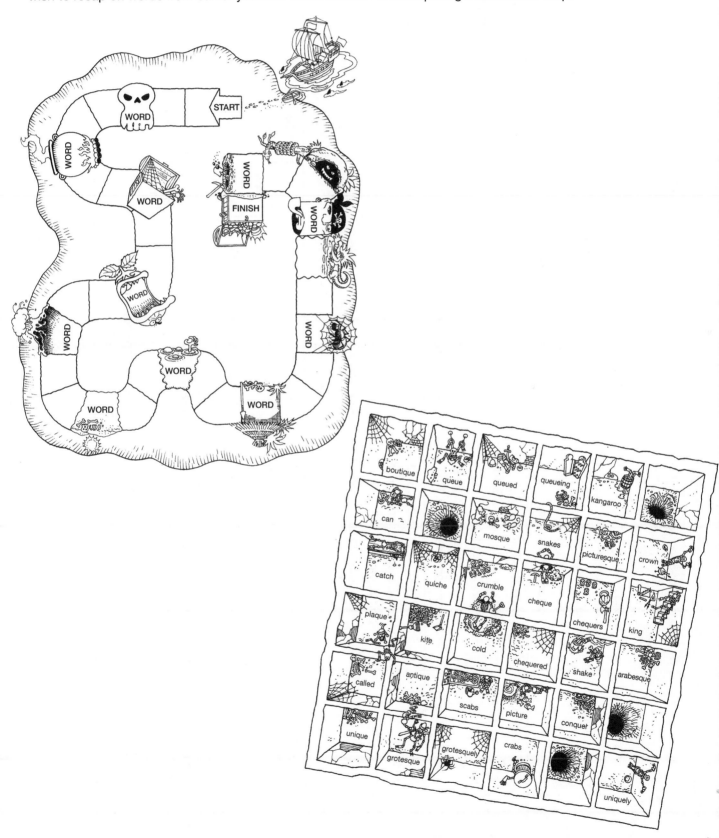

Delivering the 2014 National Curriculum for English

Unit	Title	Treasure House resources	Collins Connect	English Programme of Study	English Grammar, Punctuation and Spelling Test code
1	Adding suffixes beginning with vowels to words of more than one syllable	• Spelling Skills Pupil Book 3, Unit 1, pages 4–5 • Spelling Skills Teacher's Guide 3 – Unit 1, pages 22–23 – Photocopiable Unit 1, Resource 1: Begin at the beginning, page 75 – Photocopiable Unit 1, Resource 2: Marvellous spellings, page 76	Treasure House Spelling Year 3, Unit 1	Adding suffixes beginning with vowel letters to words of more than one syllable	S38 G6.3
2	The /i/ sound spelt y	• Spelling Skills Pupil Book 3, Unit 2, pages 6–7 • Spelling Skills Teacher's Guide 3 – Unit 2, pages 24–25 – Photocopiable Unit 2, Resource 1: The syrup story, page 77 – Photocopiable Unit 2, Resource 2: Spelling's no mystery, page 78	Treasure House Spelling Year 3, Unit 2	The /i/ sound spelt y elsewhere than at the end of words	S39
3	The /u/ sound spelt ou	• Spelling Skills Pupil Book 3, Unit 3, pages 8–9 • Spelling Skills Teacher's Guide 3 – Unit 3, pages 26–27 – Photocopiable Unit 3, Resource 1: A couple of troublesome letters, page 79 – Photocopiable Unit 3, Resource 2: Tough words to spell, page 80	Treasure House Spelling Year 3, Unit 3	The /ʌ/ sound spelt ou	S40
4	The prefixes dis– and mis–	• Spelling Skills Pupil Book 3, Unit 4, pages 10–11 • Spelling Skills Teacher's Guide 3 – Unit 4, pages 28–29 – Photocopiable Unit 4, Resource 1: I dislike misspelling, page 81 – Photocopiable Unit 4, Resource 2: Disspell or misspell? page 82	Treasure House Spelling Year 3, Unit 4	More prefixes	S41 G6.2
5	The prefixes in–, ir–, im– and il–	• Spelling Skills Pupil Book 3, Unit 5, pages 12–13 • Spelling Skills Teacher's Guide 3 – Unit 5, pages 30–31 – Photocopiable Unit 5, Resource 1: Incredible spellings, page 83 – Photocopiable Unit 5, Resource 2: Illuminating spellings, page 84	Treasure House Spelling Year 3, Unit 5	More prefixes	S41 G6.2

Unit	Title	Treasure House resources	Collins Connect	English Programme of Study	English Grammar, Punctuation and Spelling Test code

6	The prefixes re– and inter–	• Spelling Skills Pupil Book 3, Unit 6, pages 14–15
		• Spelling Skills Teacher's Guide 3
		  – Unit 6, pages 32–33
		  – Photocopiable Unit 6, Resource 1: Re and inter search, page 85
		  – Photocopiable Unit 6, Resource 2: Adding re– or inter–, page 86
			Treasure House Spelling Year 3, Unit 6	More prefixes	S41
					G6.2

7	The prefixes sub– and super–	• Spelling Skills Pupil Book 3, Unit 7, pages 16–17
		• Spelling Skills Teacher's Guide 3
		  – Unit 7, pages 34–35
		  – Photocopiable Unit 7, Resource 1: Superboy to the rescue! page 87
		  – Photocopiable Unit 7, Resource 2: Super jigsaw! page 88
			Treasure House Spelling Year 3, Unit 7	More prefixes	S41
					G6.2

8	The prefixes anti– and auto–	• Spelling Skills Pupil Book 3, Unit 8, pages 18–19
		• Spelling Skills Teacher's Guide 3
		  – Unit 8, pages 36–37
		  – Photocopiable Unit 8, Resource 1: Auto– or anti–: matching meanings, page 89
		  – Photocopiable Unit 8, Resource 2: The antidote to spelling mistakes, page 90
			Treasure House Spelling Year 3, Unit 8	More prefixes	S41
					G6.2

9	The suffix –ation	• Spelling Skills Pupil Book 3, Unit 9, pages 22–23
		• Spelling Skills Teacher's Guide 3
		  – Unit 9, pages 39–40
		  – Photocopiable Unit 9, Resource 1: Verb to noun transformations, page 91
		  – Photocopiable Unit 9, Resource 2: An exploration of the suffix –ation, page 92
			Treasure House Spelling Year 3, Unit 9	The suffix –ation	S42

Unit	Title	Treasure House resources	Collins Connect	English Programme of Study	English Grammar, Punctuation and Spelling Test code
10	Adding the suffix –ly to words ending with y	• Spelling Skills Pupil Book 3, Unit 10, pages 24–25 • Spelling Skills Teacher's Guide 3 – Unit 10, pages 41–42 – Photocopiable Unit 10, Resource 1: Hopefully using –ly easily, page 93 – Photocopiable Unit 10, Resource 2: Spelling competently and confidently, page 94	Treasure House Spelling Year 3, Unit 10	The suffix –ly	S43 G6.3
11	The ending –sure	• Spelling Skills Pupil Book 3, Unit 11, pages 26–27 • Spelling Skills Teacher's Guide 3 – Unit 11, pages 43–44 – Photocopiable Unit 11, Resource 1: Forbidden treasure, page 95 – Photocopiable Unit 11, Resource 2: Get the measure of spelling –sure, page 96	Treasure House Spelling Year 3, Unit 11	Words with endings sounding like /ʒə/ or /tʃə/	S44
12	The ending –ture	• Spelling Skills Pupil Book 3, Unit 12, pages 28–29 • Spelling Skills Teacher's Guide 3 – Unit 12, pages 45–46 – Photocopiable Unit 12, Resource 1: Sort it out: –ture, –cher or –tcher, page 97 – Photocopiable Unit 12, Resource 2: A spelling adventure, page 98	Treasure House Spelling Year 3, Unit 12	Words with endings sounding like /ʒə/ or /tʃə/	S44
13	The ending –sion	• Spelling Skills Pupil Book 3, Unit 13, pages 30–31 • Spelling Skills Teacher's Guide 3 – Unit 13, pages 47–48 – Photocopiable Unit 13, Resource 1: A spelling explosion! page 99 – Photocopiable Unit 13, Resource 2: A difficult decision: –tion or –sion? page 100	Treasure House Spelling Year 3, Unit 13	Endings which sound like /ʒən/	S45

Unit	Title	Treasure House resources	Collins Connect	English Programme of Study	English Grammar, Punctuation and Spelling Test code
14	The suffix –ous	• Spelling Skills Pupil Book 3, Unit 14, pages 32–33 • Spelling Skills Teacher's Guide 3 – Unit 14, pages 49–50 – Photocopiable Unit 14, Resource 1: Advantageous –ous words, page 101 – Photocopiable Unit 14, Resource 2: Spelling numerous –ous words, page 102	Treasure House Spelling Year 3, Unit 14	The suffix –ous	S46
15	The endings –tion, –sion and –cian	• Spelling Skills Pupil Book 3, Unit 15, pages 34–35 • Spelling Skills Teacher's Guide 3 – Unit 15, pages 51–52 – Photocopiable Unit 15, Resource 1: Be a spelling magician, page 103 – Photocopiable Unit 15, Resource 2: An education in word extension, page 104	Treasure House Spelling Year 3, Unit 15	Endings which sound like /ʃən/, spelt –tion, –sion, –ssion, –cian	S47
16	The /k/ sound spelt ch	• Spelling Skills Pupil Book 3, Unit 16, pages 36–37 • Spelling Skills Teacher's Guide 3 – Unit 16, pages 53–54 – Photocopiable Unit 16, Resource 1: School bingo, page 105 – Photocopiable Unit 16, Resource 2: Improve your spelling technique, page 106	Treasure House Spelling Year 3, Unit 16	Words with the /k/ sound spelt ch (Greek in origin)	S48
17	The /sh/ sound spelt ch	• Spelling Skills Pupil Book 3, Unit 17, pages 38–39 • Spelling Skills Teacher's Guide 3 – Unit 17, pages 55–56 – Photocopiable Unit 17, Resource 1: Be a spelling machine! page 107 – Photocopiable Unit 17, Resource 2: Lunch at the chalet, page 108	Treasure House Spelling Year 3, Unit 17	Words with the /ʃ/ sound spelt ch (mostly French in origin)	S49

Unit	Title	Treasure House resources	Collins Connect	English Programme of Study	English Grammar, Punctuation and Spelling Test code
18	The sound /k/ spelt –que and the sound /g/ spelt –gue	• Spelling Skills Pupil Book 3, Unit 18, pages 42–43 • Spelling Skills Teacher's Guide 3 – Unit 18, pages 58–59 – Photocopiable Unit 18, Resource 1: A unique challenge, page 109 – Photocopiable Unit 18, Resource 2: A catalogue of –que and –gue words, page 110	Treasure House Spelling Year 3, Unit 18	Words ending with the /g/ sound spelt –gue and the /k/ sound spelt –que (French in origin)	S50
19	The sound /s/ spelt sc	• Spelling Skills Pupil Book 3, Unit 19, pages 44–45 • Spelling Skills Teacher's Guide 3 – Unit 19, pages 60–61 – Photocopiable Unit 19, Resource 1: Searching for scissors, page 111 – Photocopiable Unit 19, Resource 2: Spelling with sc, page 112	Treasure House Spelling Year 3, Unit 19	Words with the /s/ sound spelt sc (Latin in origin)	S51
20	The sound /ay/ spelt ei, eigh and ey	• Spelling Skills Pupil Book 3, Unit 20, pages 46–47 • Spelling Skills Teacher's Guide 3 – Unit 20, pages 62–63 – Photocopiable Unit 20, Resource 1: The aim of the game: Find words that sound the same, page 113 – Photocopiable Unit 20, Resource 2: ei, eigh and ey crossword, page 114	Treasure House Spelling Year 3, Unit 20	Words with the /eɪ/ sound spelt ei, eigh, or ey	S52
21	The possessive apostrophe with plural words	• Spelling Skills Pupil Book 3, Unit 21, pages 48–49 • Spelling Skills Teacher's Guide 3 – Unit 21, pages 64–65 – Photocopiable Unit 21, Resource 1: The nouns' apostrophes, page 115 – Photocopiable Unit 21, Resource 2: The apostrophes of the nouns, page 116	Treasure House Spelling Year 3, Unit 21	Possessive apostrophe with plural words	G5.8

Unit	Title	Treasure House resources	Collins Connect	English Programme of Study	English Grammar, Punctuation and Spelling Test code

22	Homophones and near-homophones (1)	• Spelling Skills Pupil Book 3, Unit 22, pages 50–51
		• Spelling Skills Teacher's Guide 3
		  – Unit 22, pages 66–67
		  – Photocopiable Unit 22, Resource 1: <u>Who's accepting</u> a spelling <u>medal</u>? page 117
		  – Photocopiable Unit 22, Resource 2: <u>Effect versus affect</u>, page 118
			Treasure House Spelling Year 3, Unit 22	Homophones and near-homophones	S61

23	Homophones and near-homophones (2)	• Spelling Skills Pupil Book 3, Unit 23, pages 52–53
		• Spelling Skills Teacher's Guide 3
		  – Unit 23, pages 68–69
		  – Photocopiable Unit 23, Resource 1: I've <u>heard</u> you're <u>great</u> at spelling! page 119
		  – Photocopiable Unit 23, Resource 2: 'Knot' not 'not', page 120
			Treasure House Spelling Year 3, Unit 23	Homophones and near-homophones	S61

24	Homophones and near-homophones (3)	• Spelling Skills Pupil Book 3, Unit 24, pages 54–55
		• Spelling Skills Teacher's Guide 3
		  – Unit 24, pages 70–71
		  – Photocopiable Unit 24, Resource 1: <u>Meet</u> simple words with <u>plain</u> meanings, page 121
		  – Photocopiable Unit 24, Resource 2: Spellings not to be <u>missed</u>, page 122
			Treasure House Spelling Year 3, Unit 24	Homophones and near-homophones	S61

25	Homophones and near-homophones (4)	• Spelling Skills Pupil Book 3, Unit 25, pages 56–57
		• Spelling Skills Teacher's Guide 3
		  – Unit 25, pages 72–73
		  – Photocopiable Unit 25, Resource 1: Have you <u>seen</u> these spellings? page 123
		  – Photocopiable Unit 25, Resource 2: Spellings to make or <u>break</u> you, page 124
			Treasure House Spelling Year 3, Unit 25	Homophones and near-homophones	S61

Unit 1: Adding suffixes beginning with vowels to words of more than one syllable

Overview

English curriculum objectives
- Adding suffixes beginning with vowel letters to words of more than one syllable

Treasure House resources
- Spelling Skills Pupil Book 3 Unit 1, pages 4–5
- Collins Connect Treasure House Spelling Year 3, Unit 1
- Photocopiable Unit 1 Resource 1: Begin at the beginning, page 75

- Photocopiable Unit 1 Resource 2: Marvell<u>ous</u> spell<u>ings</u>, page 76

Additional resources
- Word cards: prefer, preferred, forgot, forgotten, begin, beginning, upset, upsetting, transfer, transferred, regret, regretted, forbid, forbidden, occur, occurring, refer, referred, travel, traveller, label, labelling, cancel, cancelled, marvel, marvellous, signal, signalled, quarrel, quarrelled, open, opened, listen, listening, water, watering, allow, allowed

Introduction

Teaching overview
When adding suffixes such as '–ing', '–ed', '–en' or '–er' to words of two syllables or more, we need to know whether to double the last letter or not. If the last syllable of the root word is stressed, or ends in the letter 'l', double the last letter. For example: 'begin' → 'beginning', 'travel' → 'traveller', 'forbid' → 'forbidden'. If the last syllable of the root word is not stressed, ends with a 'w' or ends with two consonants, do not double the last consonant. For example: 'listen' → 'listened', 'allow' → 'allowed', 'present' → 'presented'. However, there are not many useful two-syllable verbs that do not double the last consonant ('open', 'listen', 'water', 'profit' and 'limit') so it might be easier to just learn these.

Introduce the concept
Give each child one of the word cards (see Additional resources) and ask them to find their partner. (Reduce the number of pairs to match your group size.) Ask them to work with their partner to decide what the root word was and how the root word has or has not changed when the suffix was added. Tell them to look at their root word and decide whether the stress is on the first or second syllable. Ask pairs to tell you their word and use each pair to explain the rule. Redistribute the cards and ask the children to find their new partner and discuss how their words fit the rule.

Pupil practice

Pupil Book pages 4–5

Get started
The children sort words into two groups: those where the last consonant of the root word is doubled and those where the last consonant is not. Afterwards, identify each root word and use the words to establish the connection between stress and whether the last letter was doubled.

Answers

Consonant not doubled		Consonant doubled	
listened	[example]	forgotten	[1 mark]
listener	[1 mark]	beginner	[1 mark]
gardener	[1 mark]	upsetting	[1 mark]
watering	[1 mark]		
gardening	[1 mark]		

Try these
The children spot the misspelt word in each sentence, write out the sentences correctly and underline the word they've corrected. Afterwards, ask the children to tell you how the word was misspelt, referring to the stress of syllables.

Answers
1. Janice <u>preferred</u> chocolate to ice cream. [example]
2. Ada had <u>forgotten</u> to buy a card for her mum. [1 mark]
3. Danu's teacher is <u>transferring</u> him from Class 1 to Class 2. [1 mark]
4. Kay was <u>beginning</u> to enjoy tennis. [1 mark]
5. Ms Hardcastle <u>presented</u> the school prizes. [1 mark]

Now try these

The children copy and complete sentences, choosing the correct spellings to fill the gaps. Afterwards, ask the children to tell you how they knew which spelling to choose.

Answers

1. *Pandora knew that she should not have opened the box.* [example]

2. It was forbidden for us to go into the forest by the school. [1 mark]
3. Frida listened carefully to the teacher's instructions. [1 mark]
4. Jo regretted not joining the cricket team at the start of term. [1 mark]
5. Hanes enjoyed playing the flute, but he was only a beginner. [1 mark]

Support, embed & challenge

Support

Use the word cards (see Additional resources) with these children. Take the root words and work out together whether they have the stress on the first or second syllable. Muddle them up and sort them into two piles: words with stress on the first syllable and words with stress on the second syllable. Repeat this exercise if necessary. Keeping them in their piles, find the '+ suffix' partner of each word. Look at the sets of words together and discuss which have the last letter of the root doubled. Emphasise the connection between where the stress is placed and the doubling of the last letter. Agree that the words ending 'l' seem to be in the wrong pile and move them to the correct pile. Point out that 'allow' seems to be in the wrong pile now and move it to the correct pile. Look at the words and check that they all fit the rule. Look at how few words are in the not doubled pile (as it has now become).

Ask the children to complete Unit 1 Resource 1: Begin at the beginning. (**Answers** The stress is on the first syllable and it doesn't end in 'l': offer, water, open; Just add '–ing': offering, watering, opening; The stress is on the second syllable or it ends in 'l': signal, forget, travel, begin; double the last letter and add '–ing': signalling, forgetting, travelling, beginning)

Embed

Organise the children into small groups and provide each group with a set of word cards (see Additional resources). Tell them to sort the word pairs into words where the final consonant is doubled and words where it isn't. Next, tell them to sort the words where the final consonant is doubled into words that have the stress on the first syllable and words that end 'l'. Tell them to take a handful of word pairs each from both piles and use them to test the rest of their group.

Ask the children to complete Unit 1 Resource 2: Marvell<u>ous</u> spell<u>ings</u>. (**Answers** quarrelled, gardening, preferred, regretted, forbidden, watered, committed, travelling, occurring, marvellous, forgotten, opening, cancelled, limited, signalling, listened, labelling)

Challenge

Provide these children with word cards of root words (see Additional resources). Ask them to add as many different suffixes as they can to each word.

Homework / Additional activities

Spelling test

Ask the children to learn one of the following lists of words for a spelling test. Challenge them to write sentences for five of the words on their list.

Core words		Support words		Challenge words	
preferred	forbidden	open	forgotten	preferred	travelling
forgotten	travelling	opened	travel	forgotten	opened
beginning	opened	allow	travelling	beginning	listened
upsetting	listened	allowed	begin	upsetting	watering
regretted	watering	forgot	beginning	regretted	occurred
				forbidden	labelling

Collins Connect: Unit 1

Ask the children to complete Unit 1 (See Teach → Year 3 → Spelling → Unit 1).

Unit 2: The /i/ sound spelt y

Overview

English curriculum objectives
- The /i/ sound spelt 'y' elsewhere than at the end of words

Treasure House resources
- Spelling Skills Pupil Book 3 Unit 2, pages 6–7
- Collins Connect Treasure House Spelling Year 3 Unit 2

- Photocopiable Unit 2 Resource 1: The syrup story page 77
- Photocopiable Unit 2 Resource 2: Spelling's no mystery, page 78

Additional resources
Word cards: gym, myth, syrup, Egypt, crystal, pyramids, oxygen, typical, bicycle, mystery, symptoms, hymn, gypsy, crypt, physics, symbol, system, Sydney, lynx, cymbal, abysmal, abyss

Introduction

Teaching overview
There are about 22 words, useful to Year 3 children, that spell the short /i/ sound with the letter 'y'. There is no pattern. The words just need to be learned.

Introduce the concept
Write the word 'gym' on the board and ask the children to help you read it. Discuss the spelling and ask if anyone knows of another word with /i/ spelt 'y'. (Perhaps someone they know has a name with this spelling.) Write the words 'gym', 'myth', 'syrup', 'Egypt', 'crystal', 'pyramids', 'oxygen', 'typical', 'bicycle', 'mystery', 'symptoms', 'hymn', 'gypsy', 'crypt', 'physics', 'symbol', 'system', 'Sydney', 'lynx', 'cymbal', 'abysmal' and 'abyss' on the board and ask volunteers to read them out. Discuss the meanings of the more unusual words. Ask the children to write the six words they think will be most useful in their writing. Give them a few minutes to memorise the words then ask them to get into pairs and test each other on spelling their chosen words.

Pupil practice

Pupil Book pages 6–7

Get started
The children write words and then locate and underline the letter 'y' in each word. Afterwards, read the words together.

Answers
1. *gym*   [example]
2. m*y*th   [1 mark]
3. s*y*rup   [1 mark]
4. Eg*y*pt   [1 mark]
5. cr*y*stal   [1 mark]
6. p*y*ramids   [1 mark]
7. ox*y*gen   [1 mark]
8. t*y*pical   [1 mark]

Try these
Ask the children to write out the sentences and underline the word that has the /i/ sound spelt 'y'.

Answers
1. *I poured some <u>syrup</u> onto my porridge.*   [example]
2. My brother was pulling a funny face in the picture – it was <u>typical</u> of him!   [1 mark]
3. Sal came up from underwater and took a big breath of <u>oxygen</u>.   [1 mark]
4. The house with the yellow door was <u>mysterious</u> and old.   [1 mark]
5. The glittering <u>crystal</u> glasses were on a silver tray.   [1 mark]
6. Naveed's family is flying all the way to <u>Egypt</u> on holiday.   [1 mark]

Now try these
The children copy and complete sentences, choosing the correct spelling of the missing word from two options.

Answers

1. *The doctor asked me about my symptoms.* *[example]*
2. The story was about a mythical beast with wings. [1 mark]
3. Carin's jumper has the school symbol on it. [1 mark]
4. Jeremy was always singing in the shower. [1 mark]
5. The distant land was ruled by a cruel king. [1 mark]

Support, embed & challenge

Support

Read the word cards with the group several times until the words are familiar (see Additional resources). Cut up the word cards and work together to recreate the words.

Read together Unit 2 Resource 1: The syrup story, checking that the children understand the story opener. Ask the children to circle the words with the 'y' for /i/ spelling. (**Answers** circle: gym, syrup, mystery, cycle, typical, cycled, crystal, cycled, system, pyramid, syrup, symbol)

Embed

Ask the children to complete Unit 2 Resource 2: Spelling's no mystery. (**Answers** correct spellings: syrup, Egypt, symbol, hideous, mix, crystal, situation, pyramid, discuss, typical, difficult, bicycle, mystery, lynx, cymbal, abysmal)

Challenge

Provide these children with a set of word cards (see Additional resources). Challenge them to write their own story, using as many words where /i/ is spelt 'y' as possible.

Homework / Additional activities

Spelling test

Ask the children to learn one of the following lists of words for a spelling test. Challenge them to write sentences for five of the words on their list.

Core words		Support words		Challenge words	
myth	crystal	gym	symbol	myth	typical
syrup	pyramid	myth	crystal	syrup	bicycle
Egypt	typical	syrup	pyramid	Egypt	mystery
symbol	bicycle	Egypt	mystery	symbol	lynx
system	mystery			system	cymbal
				crystal	abysmal
				pyramid	abyss

Collins Connect: Unit 2

Ask the children to complete Unit 2 (See Teach → Year 3 → Spelling → Unit 2).

Unit 3: The /u/ sound spelt ou

Overview

English curriculum objectives
- The /u/ sound spelt 'ou'

Treasure House resources
- Spelling Skills Pupil Book 3 Unit 3 pages 8–9
- Collins Connect Treasure House Spelling Year 3, Unit 3
- Photocopiable Unit 3 Resource 1: A couple of troublesome letters, page 79

- Photocopiable Unit 3 Resource 2: Tough words to spell, page 80

Additional resources
- Word cards: young, cousin, trouble, double, country, couple, touch, courage, rough, tough, enough
- Letter tiles: d, o, u, b, l, e, t, r, p, t, c, h, y, n, g, s, l, n, i
- A bag to put letter tiles in

Introduction

Teaching overview
The short /u/ sound is spelt 'ou' in numerous common and useful words. Three of these, 'rough', 'tough' and 'enough', have the added complication of the /f/ sound spelt 'gh'.

Introduce the concept
Write the word 'cup' on the board and underline the 'u' spelling. Ask the children to work in pairs to write down two words with the /u/ sound. Ask the children

to hold up their words. Correct any misspellings, then tell the children to read the words their classmates are holding up. Write 'young' and 'double' on the board and ask a volunteer to read the words then underline the 'ou' spelling of /u/. Write the key 'ou' words on the board: 'young', 'cousin', 'trouble', 'double', 'country', 'couple', 'touch', 'courage', 'rough', 'tough', 'enough'. Read them together and ask the children to write them down, underlining the 'ou' spelling.

Pupil practice

Pupil Book pages 8–9

Get started
The children sort words into two groups: words where 'ou' stands for /u/, and words where 'ou' doesn't stand for /u/. Afterwards, ask the children to read the words.

Answers

'ou' spells /u/		'ou' doesn't spell /u/	
young	[example]	count	[1 mark]
cousin	[1 mark]	mouth	[1 mark]
trouble	[1 mark]	noun	[1 mark]
double	[1 mark]	pound	[1 mark]

Try these
The children copy sentences and underline the words where 'ou' stands for the /u/ sound. Warn them to watch out for the 'ou' spelling of the /ow/ sound.

Afterwards, write the underlined words from the sentences on the board, sorting them into two lists: words where 'ou' spells /u/ and words where 'ou' spells /ow/ ('out', 'house', 'proud', 'clouds', 'ground', 'pounds').

Answers
1. My _younger_ brother is out playing with his friends. _[example]_
2. The new house is in the <u>countryside</u>. [1 mark]
3. Juan's <u>cousin</u> won an award – he was so proud of her! [1 mark]
4. There are a <u>couple</u> of clouds in the sky. [1 mark]
5. To score a point, just <u>touch</u> the ball to the ground. [1 mark]
6. If I do chores, I can <u>double</u> my two pounds pocket money. [1 mark]

Now try these

The children copy and complete sentences, choosing between 'ou' and 'u' to spell each missing word.

Answers

1. *The married couple went on their honeymoon.* *[example]*

2. I was in a good mood, so I was humming all the way to school. [1 mark]
3. Mr McCrury will punish us if we're late! [1 mark]
4. Jeni hopes she has the courage to sing on the stage. [1 mark]
5. Patti fell and scraped her knee on the rough step. [1 mark]

Support, embed & challenge

Support

Read each word card (see Additional resources), asking the children to sound out each phoneme. Emphasise the phoneme /u/. Give the children each one of the following cards: 'double', 'trouble', 'couple', 'touch', 'young', 'cousin'. Tell them to write their word on their whiteboard. Put the letter tiles in a bag (see Additional resources). Pull one letter out at a time and read it out. Have the children cross off the letters in their word as they hear them. The first one to cross off all the letters should shout: 'Trouble!' Hand out new words and play again.

Ask the children to complete Unit 3 Resource 1: A couple of troublesome letters. (**Answers** 1. rough, 2. trouble, 3. double, 4. touch, 5. younger, 6. cousins, 7. couple)

Embed

Ask these children to write 'ou' on the front of their whiteboards and 'u' on the back. Say a range of words with the /u/ sound in them, including the words on the word cards (see Additional resources), plus a range of /u/ spelt 'u' words, such as 'just', 'must', 'crust', 'jump', 'lump' and 'ugly'. Have the children hold up the correct spelling of /u/ for each word you say.

Ask the children to complete Unit 3 Resource 2: Tough words to spell. (**Answers** trouble, crumb, umbrella, double, upset, lump, couple, chuck, young, sung, cousin, puddle, touch, bug, rough, drummer, tough)

Challenge

Ask these children to investigate the meanings of 'flourish' and 'nourish' and to write a sentence for each.

Homework / Additional activities

Spelling test

Ask the children to learn one of the following lists of words for a spelling test. Challenge them to write sentences for five of the words on their list.

Core words		Support words		Challenge words	
trouble	touch	trouble	cousin	trouble	courage
double	courage	double	touch	double	rough
couple	rough	couple	rough	couple	tough
young	tough	young	courage	young	enough
cousin	enough			cousin	flourish
				touch	nourish

Collins Connect: Unit 3

Ask the children to complete Unit 3 (See Teach → Year 3 → Spelling → Unit 3).

Unit 4: The prefixes dis– and mis–

Overview

English curriculum objectives
- More prefixes

Treasure House resources
- Spelling Skills Pupil Book 3 Unit 4, pages 10–11
- Collins Connect Treasure House Spelling Year 3, Unit 4
- Photocopiable Unit 4 resource 1: I dislike misspelling, page 81

- Photocopiable Unit 4 resource 2: Disspell or misspell?, page 82

Additional resources
- Word cards: dis, mis, agree, appear, cover, honest, like, loyal, obey, spell, taken, place, heard, understood, behave, fortune, appointed, advantage, order

Introduction

Teaching overview

The prefixes 'mis–' and 'dis–' mean 'not', 'against' or other negations of the root word. Most words take one or the other, for example, 'disbelieve' rather than 'misbelieve', 'mistake' rather than 'distake' and learning which prefix each word takes is one of the biggest challenges for Year 3 children. When any prefix is added to a root word, there is never a change to the root word, for example, 'dis' + 'cover' → 'discover', 'mis' + 'spell' → 'misspell'. However, there are many cases where the original root word isn't easily recognisable because it is either very obscure or has fallen out of use, for example, 'disgust' and 'discuss'.

Introduce the concept

Write the words 'treat' and 'order' on the board and discuss their meanings. Now, add 'mis' and 'dis'

to create 'mistreat' and 'disorder'. Read the words together and discuss their meanings. Agree that the prefixes have created negatives of the original words. Ask: 'What has happened to the spelling of the original word?' Agree that it has stayed the same. Organise the children into groups and give each group a set of word cards (see Additional Resources). Ask them to work together to add the prefixes to the words to create new words. Explain that, in most cases, each word will only take one of the prefixes. Ask the children to list the words they have created. Afterwards, share the words, correcting any mistakes. Focus for a moment on 'misspell' and point out the double 's'. Ensure the children understand that one is from 'mis–' and one from 'spell'.

Pupil practice

Pupil Book pages 10–11

Get started

The children write out words and underline the prefixes. Afterwards, ask the children to tell you what the root word is in each case and how the prefix has changed its meaning.

Answers

1. _dis_belief		[example]
2. _mis_lead		[1 mark]
3. _dis_appear		[1 mark]
4. _mis_treat		[1 mark]
5. _dis_comfort		[1 mark]
6. _mis_place		[1 mark]
7. _dis_obey		[1 mark]
8. _mis_understand		[1 mark]

Try these

The children separate words into prefixes and root words. Afterwards, ask: 'Did the spelling of the root word change when the prefix was added? How does the prefix change the meaning of the root word?'

Answers

1. _mis / fortune_		[example]
2. dis / allow		[1 mark]
3. dis / agreement		[1 mark]
4. dis / advantage		[1 mark]
5. mis / hear		[1 mark]
6. dis / obedient		[1 mark]

Now try these

The children copy and complete sentences, choosing the correct spellings of the missing words.

Answers

1. Dasu and Ben never disagreed on which game to play. *[example]*

2. Finn was disappointed with the football result. [1 mark]

3. Amelie misheard the question. [1 mark]

4. Grace was dishonest about how much chocolate she'd had. [1 mark]

5. He made the cards disappear in a puff of smoke! [1 mark]

Support, embed & challenge

Support

Provide these children with the word cards (see Additional resources). Work with them, trying the two different prefixes on each root word. Allow time for the children to read the two possibilities and then choose the correct one. Clarify the meaning of each word, linking it to the meaning of the root word.

Ask the children to complete Unit 4 Resource 1: I dislike misspelling. (**Answers** disagree, disappear, discover, dislike; misspell, mistaken, misplace, misbehave)

Embed

Ask the children to write 'dis' at one end of their whiteboards and 'mis' at the other. Say a range of root words, including the words on the word cards (see Additional resources) plus the words 'close', 'count', 'cover', 'grace', 'guise', 'infect', 'mantle',

'pose', 'guided', 'laid' and 'read'. Have the children hold up the correct prefix for each word you say. Allow them enough time to think about their choice, encouraging them to try both possibilities in their heads before choosing 'mis' or 'dis'. Confirm the correct choice for each word, then ask a volunteer to read the new word and say its meaning.

Ask the children to complete Unit 4 Resource 2: Disspell or misspell? (**Answers** words that exist: mistaken, dislike, misunderstand, dishonest, misguided, disorder, disappear, mistake, displease, misspell, disable, mislaid, disgrace, mislead, misjudged)

Challenge

Challenge the children to predict and then check the meanings of the words 'disarm', 'misfire', 'misshapen', 'distaste' and 'dissolve'. Encourage them to write sentences to use the words.

Homework / Additional activities

Spelling test

Ask the children to learn one of the following lists of words for a spelling test. Challenge them to write sentences for five of the words on their list.

Core words		Support words		Challenge words	
disagree	disobey	disagree	misspell	disagree	disadvantage
disappear	misspell	disappear	mistaken	disappear	disappointed
discover	mistaken	discover	misplace	discover	misspell
dislike	misplace	dislike	misbehave	dislike	mistaken
dishonest	misbehave			dishonest	misplace
				disobey	misbehave

Collins Connect: Unit 4

Ask the children to complete Unit 4 (See Teach → Year 3 → Spelling → Unit 4).

Unit 5: The prefixes in–, ir–, im– and il–

Overview

English curriculum objectives
- More prefixes

Treasure House resources
- Spelling Skills Pupil Book 3 Unit 5, pages 12–13
- Collins Connect Treasure House Spelling Year 3, Unit 5
- Photocopiable Unit 5 Resource 1: Incredible spellings, page 83

- Photocopiable Unit 5 Resource 2: Illuminating spellings, page 84

Additional resources
- Word cards: in, im, il, ir, legal, logical, mature, mobile, patient, possible, practical, mortal, prison, correct, credible, accurate, experienced, responsible, regular

Introduction

Teaching overview

The prefixes 'in–', 'il–' and 'ir–' are difficult for Year 3 children. The prefix 'in–' can either create a negative or signify an intensification of the root word's meaning. The negative connotation is more common. To make matters more complicated, the spelling of this prefix changes depending on the root word: the spelling of 'in–' changes to 'il–' for words beginning 'l'; 'ir–' for words beginning 'r'; and 'im–' for words beginning 'm' or 'p'. Coming from Latin, the words that 'in–' combines with are often Latinate and more complicated. For example, the English 'un–' prefix gives us 'unbelievable' whereas the Latin 'in–' gives us 'incredible'. Time should be spent learning the meanings of the words as well as the spelling.

Introduce the concept

Write the words 'possible' and 'expensive' on the board. Ask: 'How can we make these words into their opposites?' Agree that we can add 'im–' and 'in–' to create 'impossible' and 'inexpensive'. Organise the children into groups and give each group a set of word cards (see Additional resources). Ask them to work together to add a prefix to each word. Explain that, in most cases, each word will only take one of the prefixes. Ask the children to compile a list of words using the word cards. Afterwards, share the words, correcting any mistakes. Focus for a moment on 'immobile' and point out the double 'm'. Ensure the children understand that one is from 'im–' and one from 'mobile'. Look at the spelling patterns: 'im–' is used for words beginning 'm' or 'p'; 'ir–' is used for words beginning 'r'; 'il–' is used for words beginning 'l'.

Pupil practice

Pupil Book pages 12–13

Get started

The children copy words and underline the prefixes. Afterwards, ask why the words 'illegible', 'illegal', 'irresponsible' and 'immobile' have a double letter when the others don't. Ensure the children understand that prefix ends with the same letter that the root words starts with.

Answers
1. *illegible*   *[example]*
2. impossible   [1 mark]
3. illegal   [1 mark]

4. irresponsible   [1 mark]
5. inactive   [1 mark]
6. impatient   [1 mark]
7. intolerant   [1 mark]
8. immobile   [1 mark]

Try these

The children copy words, adding a prefix to each. Recap on the rules about choosing between these prefixes. Remind them that the prefix often matches the start of the root word (and 'im–' also goes with words beginning 'p'). If not, use 'in–'.

Answers

1. *inconvenient*		*[example]*
2. incorrect		[1 mark]
3. incapable		[1 mark]
4. illiterate		[1 mark]
5. irresponsible		[1 mark]
6. incompetent		[1 mark]
7. improper		[1 mark]

Now try these

The children copy and complete sentences, choosing the correct spelling of the missing word. Ask the children to read the missing word out loud to hear if it sounds right, double checking using the rules for choosing between 'im–', 'ir–', 'il–' and 'in–'.

Answers

1. *Akhil's skiing holiday was incredible.*	*[example]*
2. Antonia found the chocolate cake irresistible!	[1 mark]
3. Christopher's handwriting was illegible.	[1 mark]
4. My brother can be so childish and immature.	[1 mark]
5. I got five incorrect answers in my maths test.	[1 mark]

Support, embed & challenge

Support

Return to the word cards with these children (see Additional resources). Ensure that the children understand the meaning of each root word before adding the appropriate prefix. Create a chart with the headings 'in', 'im', 'il' and 'ir' and list the words under each prefix.

Ask the children to complete Unit 5 Resource 1: Incredible spellings. (**Answers** words beginning 'in–': incorrect, incredible, inactive; words beginning 'im–': impatient, impossible, immature; words beginning 'ir–': irregular, irrelevant; words beginning 'il–': illogical)

Embed

Ask the children to complete Unit 5 Resource 2: Illuminating spellings. (**Answers** words that exist: irregular, irresponsible, impatient, incorrect, impossible, inadequate, insane, inexpensive, inactive, incompetent, incredible, insufficient)

Organise the children into groups and provide each group with the root word cards (see Additional resources). Challenge them to add either 'im–', 'ir–', 'il–' or 'in–' without the support of the prefix cards.

Challenge

Ask these children to investigate the meanings of the words 'import', 'export', 'immigration' and 'emigration'.

Homework / Additional activities

Spelling test

Ask the children to learn one of the following lists of words for a spelling test. Challenge them to write sentences for five of the words on their list.

Core words		Support words		Challenge words	
incorrect	impossible	incorrect	immature	incorrect	irregular
incredible	irregular	incredible	impossible	incredible	inadequate
inactive	inadequate	inactive	irregular	inactive	irresponsible
immature	insufficient			immature	insufficient
				impossible	improper

Collins Connect: Unit 5

Ask the children to complete Unit 5 (See Teach → Year 3 → Spelling → Unit 5).

Unit 6: The prefixes re–
and inter–

Overview

English curriculum objectives
- More prefixes

Treasure House resources
- Spelling Skills Pupil Book 3 Unit 6, pages 14–15
- Collins Connect Treasure House Spelling Year 3, Unit 6

- Photocopiable Unit 6 Resource 1: Re and inter search, page 85
- Photocopiable Unit 6 Resource 2: Adding re– or inter–, page 86

Additional resources
- Word cards: re, inter, place, plant, play, read, search, shape, tell, think, view, vision, city, com, net, act, national

Introduction

Teaching overview
The prefix 'inter–' means 'between'; the prefix 're–' means 'again'. As with previous prefixes, the root word does not change.

Introduce the concept
Write the word 'international' on the board. Ask: 'How would you split this word into its prefix and root word?' Agree that it is 'inter' + 'national'. Explain that the prefix 'inter–' means 'between'. Challenge the children to work in their group to come up with

a list of more words beginning 'inter–', for example, 'interfere', 'interview', 'interact', and so on. Write the words on the board and discuss the meaning of each word, emphasising the meaning of the prefix 'inter–' wherever possible. Write the word 'review' on the board and establish that this is 're' + 'view'. Explain that 're–' means 'again'. Ask the children to work in their groups to list as many words as they can beginning with 're–'. Write the words on the board and discuss the meaning of each word. Point out that 're–' is a very useful prefix and that many words begin with it.

Pupil practice

Pupil Book pages 14–15

Get started
The children copy words and underline the prefixes. Ask the children to use their understanding of the prefixes to explain the meaning of each word.

Answers
1. _interview_   _[example]_
2. <u>re</u>name   [1 mark]
3. <u>re</u>write   [1 mark]
4. <u>re</u>do   [1 mark]
5. <u>inter</u>link   [1 mark]
6. <u>inter</u>national   [1 mark]
7. <u>inter</u>action   [1 mark]
8. <u>re</u>act   [1 mark]

Try these
The children add 're–' or 'inter–' to root words. Tell them to try each option, saying the new words out loud to hear which sounds right. Remind them to use their knowledge of the meanings of the prefixes to choose the right one.

Answers
1. _revalue_   _[example]_
2. relocate   [1 mark]
3. international   [1 mark]
4. reassemble   [1 mark]
5. redial   [1 mark]
6. reclaim   [1 mark]
7. reunite   [1 mark]
8. redeliver   [1 mark]

Now try these
The children copy and complete sentences, choosing the correct prefix ('re–' or 'inter–') to complete the word.

Answers
1. _It was busy at Exeter International Airport today._   _[example]_
2. Mo waited for the rainbow to reappear.   [1 mark]
3. I need to do lots of revision for my exams.   [1 mark]
4. It was a long, slow intercity bus journey.   [1 mark]
5. Today I am going to reorganise my desk.   [1 mark]
6. The Johnsons want to relocate to a new area.   [1 mark]

Support, embed & challenge

Support

Ask these children to complete Unit 6 Resource 1: Re and inter search. (**Answers** intercity, review, intercom, restore, internet, rethink, react, remake, replace, repack, rewind)

Cut out the words from a copy of Unit 6 Resource 1: Re and inter search. As a group, sort the words according to their prefixes. Ask the children to cut the prefix off each word. Muddle up the root words and ask the children to reattach the prefixes.

Embed

Ask these children to work in small groups and give each group a set of word cards (see Additional resources). Tell the children to match prefixes and root words, and to write down all the words that they create.

Ask the children to complete Unit 6 Resource 2: Adding re– or inter–. (**Answers** 1. international, 2. repaint, 3. replant, 4. intercity, 5. internet, 6. repay)

Challenge

Ask these children to look at the words and prefixes covered over the last three units and locate words that can take more than one prefix, such as 'disappear', 'reappear', 'retake', 'mistake', 'intake', 'interview', 'review'. Challenge them to find as many of these words as they can.

Homework / Additional activities

Spelling test

Ask the children to learn one of the following lists of words for a spelling test. Challenge them to write sentences for five of the words on their list.

Core words		Support words		Challenge words	
react	reappear	react	rewrite	react	redeliver
rebuild	review	replace	intercity	rebuild	intercity
remove	intercity	remove	interfere	remove	interfere
rename	internet	rename	internet	rename	internet
rewrite	interrupt			rewrite	interrupt
				reappear	international
				review	intervene
				reassemble	

Collins Connect: Unit 6

Ask the children to complete Unit 6 (See Teach → Year 3 → Spelling → Unit 6).

Unit 7: The prefixes sub– and super–

Overview

English curriculum objectives
- More prefixes

Treasure House resources
- Spelling Skills Pupil Book 3 Unit 7, pages 16–17

- Collins Connect Treasure House Spelling Year 3, Unit 7
- Photocopiable Unit 7 Resource 1: Superboy to the rescue!, page 87
- Photocopiable Unit 7 Resource 2: Super jigsaw!, page 88

Introduction

Teaching overview
The prefix 'super–' means 'over', 'beyond' or 'greater', for example, 'superhero', 'superpowers'. The prefix 'sub–' means 'under' or 'less', for example, 'subheading', 'subordinate'.

Introduce the concept
Write the word 'superhero' on the board and ask the children to tell you about their favourite superhero.

As different children talk, note down any 'super–' words they use to describe their chosen character, for example, 'supercar', 'superpowers', 'superman', 'supervision'. Look at the words together and introduce the prefix, talking about all the nouns that the prefix 'super–' can enhance.

Move on to introduce the less exciting prefix 'sub–' and explain its meaning. Share words with this prefix, such as 'submarine', 'subheading', 'subtitle' and 'submerge'

Pupil practice

Pupil Book pages 16–17

Get started
The children copy words and underline the prefixes. Afterwards, ask: 'What root word was the suffix added to?' Discuss how the prefix changes the meaning of the root word (but not the spelling).

Answers
1. *supermarket*   *[example]*
2. submarine   [1 mark]
3. superstar   [1 mark]
4. subway   [1 mark]
5. superhuman   [1 mark]
6. superstore   [1 mark]
7. subtract   [1 mark]
8. subscribe   [1 mark]

Try these
The children copy root words then add the prefix 'sub–' or 'super–'. Tell the children to try out both prefixes with the root word, saying each new word out loud before deciding which word is the one that exists in English.

Answers
1. *subtitle*   *[example]*
2. subheading   [1 mark]
3. subdivide   [1 mark]
4. subsection   [1 mark]
5. supersize   [1 mark]
6. superman   [1 mark]
7. supervision   [1 mark]
8. submerge   [1 mark]

Now try these
The children copy and complete sentences by adding the missing prefix 'sub–' or 'super–'. Afterwards, discuss the meanings of the words they completed. Clarify the meanings of 'subdued' and 'submariner'. Ask the children to infer the nature of the person lifting the car in the third sentence.

Answers
1. *The new supermarket opened last week.* *[example]*
2. The atmosphere at the match was subdued.   [1 mark]

3. He lifted the car with superhuman strength. [1 mark]

4. Never use sharp knives without supervision. [1 mark]

5. Janice cancelled her subscription to the magazine. [1 mark]

6. The submariners lived aboard their submarine. [1 mark]

Support, embed & challenge

Support

Ask these children to complete Unit 7 Resource 1: Superboy to the rescue! (**Answers** circle: Superboy, subway, supermarket, supersonic, supersensitive, submarine, submarine, submerged, superhuman, Superboy, Superboy)

Afterwards, read the story together and decide what is going to happen next. Talk about what gadgets might help Superboy and any new superhero characters that could be introduced. Together, write the rest of the story, using as many 'super–' words as possible.

Embed

Ask these children to complete Unit 7 Resource 2: Super jigsaw! (**Answers** submarine, superhero, subheading, supersize, subtitle, superstar, submerge, substandard, supervision, subsection, superpower, subtract, subway, superstore, subscribe)

Ask the children to create a superhero comic strip. Tell them to write a caption for each picture, challenging them to use the words 'submarine', 'submerge', 'subway' and as many 'super–' words as they can.

Challenge

Ask these children to write a story using the words 'submarine', 'submerge', 'subway', 'subdued', 'subsequent' and as many 'super–' words as they can. Challenge them to find out the meaning of the word 'subconscious'.

Homework / Additional activities

Spelling test

Ask the children to learn one of the following lists of words for a spelling test. Challenge them to write sentences for five of the words on their list.

Core words		Support words		Challenge words	
supermarket	subheading	supermarket	subheading	supermarket	submarine
superhero	subtitle	superhero	subtitle	superhero	submerge
superpower	submarine	superpower	submarine	superpower	subtitle
superstar	submerge	supersonic	subway	superstar	subway
supersonic	subway			supersonic	subdued
				superintendent	subsequent
				subheading	

Collins Connect: Unit 7

Ask the children to complete Unit 7 (See Teach → Year 3 → Spelling → Unit 7).

Unit 8: The prefixes anti– and auto–

Overview

English curriculum objectives
- More prefixes

Treasure House resources
- Spelling Skills Pupil Book 3 Unit 8, pages 18–19
- Collins Connect Treasure House Spelling Year 3, Unit 8
- Photocopiable Unit 8 Resource 1: Auto– or anti–: matching meanings, page 89

- Photocopiable Unit 8 Resource 2: The antidote to spelling mistakes, page 90

Additional resources
- Word cards: antibacterial, antibiotics, anticlimax, anticlockwise, antidote, antifreeze, antihero, antiseptic, antisocial, antiserum, autobiography, autograph, automatic, automobile, autopilot

Introduction

Teaching overview
The prefix 'anti–' means 'against'. The words that start with this prefix are, in the main, rather difficult for Year 3 children. But there are a small number that they will be able to use.

The prefix 'auto–' means 'oneself'. There are only five words with the prefix 'auto–' that are suitable for use in Year 3: 'autobiography', 'autograph', 'automatic', 'autopilot' and, perhaps, 'automobile'.

Introduce the concept
Create two sets of the words cards (see Additional resources) and give a few words to each group.

Ask them to work in their groups to decide what the prefixes 'anti–' and 'auto–' might mean. Listen to their ideas and correct any misapprehensions. Next, ask the children to use their understanding of the prefixes 'anti–' and 'auto–' to work out what the words on the word cards mean. Share all the words and confirm their meanings. Explain that an 'antihero' is an unlikely hero: the main character of a story who has little or nothing hero-like about them.

Pupil practice

Pupil Book pages 18–19

Get started
The children copy words and underline the prefixes. After the children have written the words, ask them to tell you what each word means, using the meaning of the prefixes and root words to help. For example, 'antisocial' is something that is against good social behaviour, an 'automobile' is something that moves on its own.

Answers
1. *automatic*	*[example]*
2. anticlockwise	[1 mark]
3. antiseptic	[1 mark]
4. automobile	[1 mark]
5. antisocial	[1 mark]
6. antibiotics	[1 mark]

Try these
The children copy words and add the prefixes 'anti–' or 'auto–'. Tell the children to try out both prefixes with the root word, saying each new word out loud before deciding which word is the one that exists in English. Afterwards, discuss the meaning of 'anticlimax' using the meaning of the prefix and root word. Discuss the meaning of 'antihero'. Clarify that it is not the villain but the main character, or hero, of a story who isn't very hero-like.

Answers
1. *autograph*	*[example]*
2. anticlimax	[1 mark]
3. autopilot	[1 mark]
4. antifreeze	[1 mark]
5. antihero	[1 mark]
6. anticlockwise	[1 mark]

Now try these

The children copy and complete the sentences by writing the missing prefixes. After the children have chosen the prefixes, read the sentences together ensuring that the children understand the meaning of each. Take the opportunity to discuss the difference between 'unsociable' and 'antisocial'.

Answers

1. *For some spider bites there is no antidote.*

[example]

2. The band signed autographs as they left the concert. [1 mark]

3. Littering and drawing graffiti are antisocial activities. [1 mark]

4. What a life she has led! She should write an autobiography. [1 mark]

5. I cleaned his cuts and grazes with antibacterial wipes. [1 mark]

6. The end of the film was a disappointing anticlimax. [1 mark]

Support, embed & challenge

Support

With these children, read a selection of word cards with the most straightforward words: 'autograph', 'autopilot', 'autobiography', 'automatic', 'antifreeze', 'anticlockwise'. Cut each word up into root word and prefix. Muddle up the cards and work together to recreate the words. Discuss the meaning of each word created.

Ask the children to complete Unit 8 Resource 1: Auto– or anti–: matching meanings. (**Answers** 1. anticlockwise, 2. autobiography, 3. autograph, 4. antifreeze, 5. automatic, 6. antidote, 7. autopilot)

Embed

Ask these children to complete Unit 8 Resource 2: The antidote to spelling mistakes. (**Answers** 1. anticlockwise, 2. autobiography, 3. automobile, 4. autograph, 5. antifreeze, 6. antidote, 7. autopilot, 8. antisocial, 9. antibacterial, 10. anticlimax)

Organise the children into groups of four and provide each group with a set of word cards (see Additional resources). Edit the word card sets to suit the ability of each group. Tell the groups to work in teams of two. One child should pick a card and describe the word to their team mate for them to guess. If they guess correctly, their team keeps the card. If they don't guess correctly, the other team can try to guess, and will keep the card if they are correct. If no one guesses the word, the card is returned to the pack. The teams should take turns to pick a card and describe and guess the word. Teams should also alternate describers and guessers.

Challenge

Ask these children to think of the main characters of their favourite stories and decide if any of them could be called an antihero.

Homework / Additional activities

Spelling test

Ask the children to learn one of the following lists of words for a spelling test. Challenge them to write sentences for five of the words on their list.

Core words		Support words		Challenge words	
anticlockwise	autobiography	anticlockwise	antisocial	anticlockwise	autograph
antifreeze	autograph	antifreeze	autobiography	antifreeze	automatic
antidote	automatic	antidote	autograph	antidote	antibacterial
antiseptic	autopilot	antiseptic	automatic	antiseptic	antibiotics
antisocial	anticlimax			antisocial	antihero
				autobiography	

Collins Connect: Unit 8

Ask the children to complete Unit 8 (See Teach → Year 3 → Spelling → Unit 8).

Review unit 1

Pupil Book pages 20–21

A. Ask children to add the suffix or prefix to each word. Remind children that sometimes they'll need to double the last letter before adding the suffix.

1. numbered [1 mark]
2. admitted [1 mark]
3. targeting [1 mark]
4. beginner [1 mark]
5. rewrite [1 mark]
6. international [1 mark]
7. rename [1 mark]
8. replace [1 mark]
9. anticlockwise [1 mark]
10. autopilot [1 mark]
11. supermarket [1 mark]
12. sublevel [1 mark]

B. Ask children to choose the correct spelling.

1. myth [1 mark]
2. pyramid [1 mark]
3. crystal [1 mark]
4. Egypt [1 mark]
5. cousin [1 mark]
6. touch [1 mark]
7. double [1 mark]
8. trouble [1 mark]

C. Ask children to use the prefixes dis–, mis–, il–, im–, in– and ir– to write the opposites of the words.

1. disappear [1 mark]
2. disobey [1 mark]
3. misspell [1 mark]
4. misunderstand [1 mark]
5. illegal [1 mark]
6. impossible [1 mark]
7. incorrect [1 mark]
8. irregular [1 mark]

Unit 9: The suffix –ation

Overview

English curriculum objectives

- The suffix –ation

Treasure House resources

- Spelling Skills Pupil Book 3 Unit 9, pages 22–23
- Collins Connect Treasure House Spelling Year 3, Unit 9
- Photocopiable Unit 9 Resource 1: Verb to noun transformations, page 91

- Photocopiable Unit 9 Resource 2: An exploration of the suffix –ation, page 92

Additional resources

- Word cards: inform, adore, sense, prepare, admire, limit, inspire, explore, observe, compile, reserve, conserve, determine, organise, examine, continue

Introduction

Teaching overview

The suffix '–ation' can be used to turn verbs into nouns, for example, 'prepare' → 'preparation'. The suffix can be added directly to some verbs, such as 'inform' → 'information'. However, in some cases, a final 'e' needs to be removed, for example, 'admire' → 'admiration'. There are many words ending in '–ation' where the root word has changed in other ways. However, this unit focuses on words where the verb → noun relationship is straightforward.

Introduce the concept

Write the words 'prepare' and 'preparation' on the board. Ask the children to help you make up a sentence for each, for example: 'The girls prepare a fruit salad.' 'The preparation for the show was hard work.' Help the children to see that 'prepare' is a verb and 'preparation' a noun. Use the words 'organise', 'inform', 'observe' and 'admire' to demonstrate the spelling rules, showing when to remove the final 'e'.

Pupil practice

Pupil Book pages 22–23

Get started

The children look at the words in the list and decide which are spelt correctly and which are not. They write the ones that are spelt correctly in the first column of a table and write the correct spellings of the words that are spelt wrongly in the second column.

Answers

Correctly spelt words		Corrected words	
formation	*[example]*	continuation	[1 mark]
continuation	[1 mark]	sensation	[1 mark]
sensation	[1 mark]	admiration	[1 mark]
admiration	[1 mark]	determination	[1 mark]

Try these

The children add '–ation' to verbs to create nouns. Remind the children that, if the root verb ends in an 'e', they must remove the 'e' before adding '–ation'. Discuss the meanings of the new words, making up sentences together.

Answers

1. *limitation*		*[example]*
2. inspiration		[1 mark]
3. exploration		[1 mark]
4. observation		[1 mark]
5. compilation		[1 mark]
6. reservation		[1 mark]

Now try these

The children copy and complete sentences by adding '–ation' to one verb in each sentence. Ask the children to read each sentence and find the word that sounds wrong. Explain that these words are verbs when they should be nouns. Remind children that they might need to remove the 'e' from the verb first.

Answers

1. *The children read the information on the poster.*
                                          [example]

2. Rahul was full of admiration for his hero.   [1 mark]

3. Carl made a reservation at the restaurant.   [1 mark]

4. Anika makes an observation of rare birds.   [1 mark]

5. We should support the conservation of wildlife.   [1 mark]

6. Oscar studied hard in preparation for his exams.   [1 mark]

Support, embed & challenge

Support

Ask the children to cut out the words on Unit 9 Resource 1: Verb to noun transformations. Have the children sort the words into pairs of related verbs and nouns. Look at each verb and ask the children to decide if its meaning changed when the '–ation' ending was added. Discuss how the addition of '–ation' changes the meaning. Create sentences for the pairs of words to illustrate the change from verb to noun.

Organise the children into pairs and instruct them to use the words from the resource sheet to play a game of 'Pairs' where they match the related verbs and nouns. (**Answers** pairs: inform, information; observe, observation; adore, adoration; determine, determination; prepare, preparation; organise, organisation; inspire, inspiration; examine, examination; explore, exploration; converse, conversation)

Embed

Organise the children into pairs and provide each pair with a set of word cards (see Additional resources). Tell them to place the cards face down and to take turns to turn one over. In their pairs, the children should race each other to write the related noun of the word they turned over.

Ask the children to complete Unit 9 Resource 2: An exploration of the suffix –ation. (**Answers** 1. observation, 2. conservation, 3. inspiration, 4. preparation, 5. organise, 6. information, 7. examination, 8. continuation)

Challenge

Challenge these children to compose sentences for the words: 'admiration', 'conservation' and 'determination'.

Homework / Additional activities

Spelling test

Ask the children to learn one of the following lists of words for a spelling test. Challenge them to write sentences for five of the words on their list.

Core words		Support words		Challenge words	
information	conversation	inform	exploration	information	conservation
preparation	observation	information	examine	preparation	determination
exploration	conservation	prepare	examination	exploration	inspiration
examination	determination	preparation	organise	examination	admiration
organisation	inspiration	explore	organisation	organisation	limitation
				conversation	reservation
				observation	

Collins Connect: Unit 9

Ask the children to complete Unit 9 (See Teach → Year 3 → Spelling → Unit 9).

Unit 10: Adding the suffix –ly to words ending with y

Overview

English curriculum objectives
- The suffix '–ly'

Treasure House resources
- Spelling Skills Pupil Book 3 Unit 10, pages 24–25
- Collins Connect Treasure House Spelling Year 3, Unit 10
- Photocopiable Unit 10 Resource 1: Hopefully using –ly easily, page 93

- Photocopiable Unit 10 Resource 2: Spelling competently and confidently, page 94

Additional resources
- Word cards: ly, i, wide, like, safe, hopeless, tireless, endless, guilty, moody, gloomy, wrinkle, wobble, bubble, gentle, tremble, possible, horrible
- Adhesive putty for sticking the 'i' card over 'y' endings

Introduction

Teaching overview
In Year 2, the children practised adding '–ly' to words that end in 'y', such as 'cheery' → 'cheerily'. In Year 3 and Year 4, the children need to become more secure with this and also learn to add '–ly' to words that end in 'le' and 'ic'. There are four rules for adding '–ly'.

1. For most words, just add '–ly', for example, 'careful' → 'carefully', 'kind' → 'kindly', 'polite' → 'politely'. Care must be taken to retain the final 'l' or final 'e' in root words.
2. For words ending in 'y', remove the 'y' and add 'i', for example, 'grumpy' → 'grumpily'.
3. For words ending in 'le', remove the 'le', for example, 'wrinkle' → 'wrinkly'.
4. For words ending in 'ic', add 'ally', for example, 'automatic' → 'automatically'.

The Pupil Book and Collins Connect activities concentrate on practising Rule 2. The Support, embed & challenge activities and Unit 10 Resource 2 provide practice for all four rules.

Introduce the concept
Recap on adding '–ly' to words such as 'kind', 'warm', 'local', 'beautiful', 'polite' and 'definite' where the root word does not change. Discuss the adverbs created. Point out the double 'l' in 'locally' and 'beautifully' and the retained 'e' in 'politely' and 'definitely'. Remind the children about the rule they learned in Year 2 for adding '–ly' to words ending in 'y'. Write 'busy', 'happy', 'hasty', 'messy' and 'easy' on the board and ask the children to work in pairs to write the adverb related to each word.

Pupil practice

Pupil Book pages 24–25

Get started
The children copy words and underline the suffix '–ly'. After the children have underlined the '–ly' endings, read the part of the word they have not underlined together and agree that it is the original root word, just spelt differently.

Answers
1. *sleepily*   [example]
2. prettily   [1 mark]
3. breezily   [1 mark]
4. cheekily   [1 mark]
5. messily   [1 mark]
6. shakily   [1 mark]
7. angrily   [1 mark]
8. hungrily   [1 mark]

Try these
The children copy words and add the suffix '–ly'. Remind the children that they will need to change the spelling of the root word.

Answers
1. *nastily*   [example]
2. hastily   [1 mark]
3. readily   [1 mark]
4. grumpily   [1 mark]
5. busily   [1 mark]
6. easily   [1 mark]

Now try these

The children copy and complete sentences by choosing the correct spellings of the missing words. Afterwards, ask them to tell you how they knew which word was spelt correctly. Discuss what the original root word would have been.

Answers

1. *The man tucked into the hamburger hungrily.*

[example]

2. The visitor was dressed shabbily. [1 mark]

3. The boy wrote shakily on the form. [1 mark]

4. The man walked to his car happily. [1 mark]

5. The thief left the building hastily. [1 mark]

6. The racing car zoomed noisily around the corner. [1 mark]

Support, embed & challenge

Support

Provide these children with word cards for the words 'wide', 'like', 'safe', 'hopeless', 'tireless', 'endless', 'guilty', 'moody' and 'gloomy', plus a card for 'ly' and a card for 'i' with adhesive putty on the back (see Additional resources). Discuss how each adjective can be turned into an adverb, ensuring the children remember that the words ending 'y' ('guilty', 'moody' and 'gloomy') need the 'y' changed for an 'i' before '–ly' is added. Stick the 'i' card over the 'y' each time to demonstrate this. Gather in the root adjectives, leaving the 'ly' and 'i' cards in the middle of the table. Give each child one of the root adjectives and ask them to locate the word parts they need to create the adverb. Explain that they might only need the word in their hand plus '–ly' or they might need to use the 'i' card to change the word first.

Ask the children to complete Unit 10 Resource 1: Hopefully using –ly easily. Afterwards, discuss the changes made to the root adjectives. Locate words that retained their final 'e' or 'l'. (**Answers** shakily, readily, truthfully, politely, uneasily, painfully, locally, tidily; endless, hopeful, funny, greedy, crazy, dreamy, kind, unkind)

Embed

Describe the spelling rule for adding '–ly' to words ending in 'le': remove the 'le' and add '–ly'. Write the words 'wrinkle', 'wobble', 'bubble', 'gentle', 'tremble', 'possible' and 'horrible' on the board. Ask the children to apply the spelling rule to add '–ly' to each word and write the new words as a list. Discuss the meaning of each new word and its relationship with its root word.

Ask the children to complete Unit 10 Resource 2: Spelling competently and confidently. (**Answers** ordinarily, beautifully, steadily, childishly, painfully, horribly, entirely, hopelessly, hopefully, smartly, healthily, largely, feebly, wobbly, closely, luckily, speedily, definitely, carefully)

Challenge

Provide these children with the words 'automatic', 'logic', 'specific', 'dramatic' and 'critic'. Ask them to discuss what the adverb related to each of these might be. Provide them with the spelling rule for adding '–ly' to words ending in 'ic' (add 'ally') and ask them to write the adverb related to each word you gave them.

Homework / Additional activities

Spelling test

Ask the children to learn one of the following lists of words for a spelling test. Challenge them to write sentences for five of the words on their list.

Core words		Support words		Challenge words	
busy busily	logic logically	easy easily	sleepy sleepily	angry angrily	crumble crumbly
noisy noisily	basic basically	busy busily	lucky luckily	breezy breezily	logic logically
lazy lazily	beautiful beautifully	happy happily	lazy lazily	grumpy grumpily	basic basically
clumsy clumsily	careful carefully	noisy noisily		gentle gently	beautiful beautifully
simple simply				simple simply	careful carefully
tickle tickly				tickle tickly	

Collins Connect: Unit 10

Ask the children to complete Unit 10 (See Teach → Year 3 → Spelling → Unit 10).

Unit 11: The ending –sure

Overview

English curriculum objectives
• Words with endings sounding like /zhur/ and /cher/

Treasure House resources
• Spelling Skills Pupil Book 3 Unit 11, pages 26–27
• Collins Connect Treasure House Spelling Year 3, Unit 11

• Photocopiable Unit 11 Resource 1: Forbidden trea<u>sure</u>, page 95
• Photocopiable Unit 11 Resource 2: Get the mea<u>sure</u> of spelling –sure, page 96

Additional resources
• Word cards: closure, composure, disclosure, displeasure, enclosure, exposure, leisure, measure, pleasure, treasure

Introduction

Teaching overview

There are a few words in English that end in a buzzy /zhur/ sound, for example, 'treasure' and 'measure'. This ending is almost always spelt 'sure' and needs to be distinguished from the /sher/ ending which is usually spelt 'sher' as in 'blusher' or 'dishwasher'. There are four words that slightly confuse this rule: 'assure', 'reassure' and 'pressure' which have the /sher/ ending spelt 'ssure', and 'insure' which has a /shor/ ending spelt 'sure'. (However, these are not very useful words for Year 3, so can be passed over at this stage).

Introduce the concept

Draw a picture of a treasure chest. Ask the children what it is. Ask the children to sound out the word

'treasure', one phoneme at a time. Pause to discuss the buzzy /zh/ sound, which is slightly different from the /sh/ sound. Ask if anyone knows how to spell 'treasure'. Write the word, pointing out /e/ spelt 'ea' and /zhur/ spelt 'sure'. Compare the ending of 'treasure' with the ending of the word 'blusher', asking the children to say 'treasure' and 'blusher' alternately. Say a range of words with both the /sher/ ending and the /zhur/ ending, for example, 'measure', 'dishwasher', 'leisure', 'fisher', 'closure', 'fresher' and 'exposure'. Ask the children to put up their hand if they hear a /zhur/ ending, allowing time for them to say it to themselves, comparing it with 'blusher'. Write each word in turn, grouping the two endings. Point out the 'sure' spelling and explain that, if they hear a /zhur/ ending, it's almost always spelt 'sure'.

Pupil practice

Pupil Book pages 26–27

Get started

The children copy words and underline the '–sure' endings.

Answers
1. trea<u>sure</u>   *[example]*
2. lei<u>sure</u>   [1 mark]
3. clo<u>sure</u>   [1 mark]
4. plea<u>sure</u>   [1 mark]
5. enclo<u>sure</u>   [1 mark]
6. mea<u>sure</u>   [1 mark]
7. expo<u>sure</u>   [1 mark]
8. disclo<u>sure</u>   [1 mark]

Try these

The children correct misspelt words. Tell the children to remember the '–sure' spelling pattern for the /zhur/ sound. Tell them to read the misspelt words and replace the incorrect spelling of /zhur/.

Answers
1. *composure*   *[example]*
2. displeasure   [1 mark]
3. exposure   [1 mark]
4. leisure   [1 mark]
5. closure   [1 mark]
6. disclosure   [1 mark]

Now try these

The children compose sentences for the target words 'measure', 'treasure', 'displeasure', 'leisure' and 'pleasure'. Ensure that the children understand the meaning of each word. Suggest they share ideas with a partner before attempting to write their sentence.

Answers

1. *Bess fed the puppies in the enclosure. [example]*

Accept sentences in which the target word is spelt correctly.   [5 marks: 1 per sentence]

Support, embed & challenge

Support

Work with these children on understanding the meaning of each word. Read the word cards with the children (see Additional resources), emphasising the 'sure' ending. Place the cards in the centre of the group and give the definition for each word, challenging the children to be the first to pick up the corresponding card.

Ask the children to complete Unit 11 Resource 1: Forbidden trea<u>sure</u>. (**Answers** circle: leisure, enclosure, measure, treasures, pleasure, displeasure, exposure, composure, disclosure)

Embed

Organise the children into pairs and provide each pair with two copies of Unit 11 Resource 2: Get the mea<u>sure</u> of spelling –sure. Ask the children to cut out the words and use them to play a game of 'Pairs'. Tell them that when they find a pair, their partner must take the pair and only give it back when the first child has correctly spelt the word.

Challenge

Challenge these children to learn the exceptions to this spelling rule: 'insure', 'pressure', 'assure' and 'reassure'.

Homework / Additional activities

Spelling test

Ask the children to learn one of the following lists of words for a spelling test. Challenge them to write sentences for five of the words on their list.

Core words	Support words	Challenge words
closure	closure	closure
composure	leisure	composure
disclosure	measure	disclosure
displeasure	pleasure	displeasure
enclosure	treasure	enclosure
exposure	exposure	exposure
leisure		leisure
measure		measure
pleasure		pleasure
treasure		treasure
		assure
		reassure
		pressure
		insure

Collins Connect: Unit 11

Ask the children to complete Unit 11 (See Teach → Year 3 → Spelling → Unit 11).

Unit 12: The ending –ture

Overview

English curriculum objectives
- Words with endings sounding like /zhur/ and /cher/

Treasure House resources
- Spelling Skills Pupil Book 3 Unit 12, pages 28–29
- Collins Connect Treasure House Spelling Year 3, Unit 12
- Photocopiable Unit 12 Resource 1: Sort it out: –ture, –cher or –tcher, page 97
- Photocopiable Unit 12 Resource 2: A spelling adventure, page 98

Additional resources
- Word cards: mixture, departure, capture, adventure, nature, picture, future, creature, feature, temperature, furniture, miniature, puncture, moisture, vulture, butcher, thatcher, catcher, snatcher, pitcher, watcher, stretcher, teacher, voucher, archer, richer, searcher, marcher
- Adhesive putty for sticking word cards to the board
- Dice and counters for groups of four to complete Unit 12 Resource 2: A spelling adventure

Introduction

Teaching overview
The /cher/ sound at the end of a word can be spelt '–cher', '–tcher' or '–ture'. The three endings are equally common in English, though the words with '–ture' are possibly more useful. The children should be aware that they are making a choice between these three endings when writing.

Introduce the concept
Hand out a word card to each child (see Additional resources). Encourage each child to read their word card in turn. Ask the children if they can tell you what sound the words have in common. Ask: 'How do we spell the /cher/ sound?' Write the three spelling patterns as headings for three columns on the board. Tell the children to decide what pattern their word has. Ask them to compare their card with the cards of two other children. Invite the children to come up to the board, one at a time, and stick their word card on the board under the correct heading. Read the words together. Point out that the words ending in '–er' comprise a root words with an '–er' suffix, for example, 'rich' + 'er'.

Pupil practice

Pupil Book pages 28–29

Get started
The children copy words and underline the '–ture' endings. Ask the children to read each word, ensuring that they can hear the /cher/ sound.

Answers
1. *furni<u>ture</u>*	*[example]*
2. cap<u>ture</u>	[1 mark]
3. vul<u>ture</u>	[1 mark]
4. crea<u>ture</u>	[1 mark]
5. na<u>ture</u>	[1 mark]
6. adven<u>ture</u>	[1 mark]
7. punc<u>ture</u>	[1 mark]
8. rup<u>ture</u>	[1 mark]

Try these
The children correct misspelt words. Tell them that each one ends /cher/ and they need to work out which part of the word should be replaced with '–ture'.

Answers
1. *picture*	*[example]*
2. moisture	[1 mark]
3. temperature	[1 mark]
4. future	[1 mark]
5. fracture	[1 mark]
6. posture	[1 mark]

Now try these
The children compose sentences for the target words 'nature', 'capture', 'picture', 'adventure' and 'pastures'. Ensure the children understand the meaning of 'pastures'.

Answers
1. *Bears are woodland creatures.* *[example]*

Accept sentences in which the target word is spelt correctly. [5 marks: 1 per sentence]

Support, embed & challenge

Support

Look at the words on Unit 12 Resource 1: Sort it out: –ture, –cher or –tcher together and discuss the endings. Ask the children to complete the activity. (**Answers** /cher/ spelt –'cher': archer, scorcher, bencher, voucher, searcher, teacher, richer, researcher; /cher/ spelt '–tcher': thatcher, snatcher, catcher, watcher, pitcher, stretcher, butcher; /cher/ spelt '–ture': nature, feature, creature, departure, puncture, future, furniture, mixture, adventure, capture, vulture, picture, temperature, moisture, miniature)

Take a fresh copy of Unit 12 Resource 1: Sort it out: –ture, –cher or –tcher and cut out the words. Work with the children to cut 'er' off the words ending '–tcher' and –cher'. Once the 'er' endings have been removed, read the root words that are left: 'arch', 'vouch', 'teach', 'search', 'rich', 'scorch', 'bench', 'research', 'thatch', 'snatch', 'catch', 'watch', 'pitch', 'stretch' and 'butch'. Work together to reattach the 'er' endings and read the words. Read the words ending '–ture' again. Point out that, if the '–ture' endings were removed, they wouldn't leave whole words. Practise reading and writing the most useful words from the resource sheet.

Embed

Organise these children into groups of four and provide each group with a set of word cards (see Additional resources). Adjust the number of cards and complexity of the vocabulary according to the abilities of the groups. Tell the children to spend time practising the spelling of each word.

Next, provide each group of four with a dice, counters and a copy of Unit 12 Resource 2: A spelling adventure and ask them to play the game.

Challenge

Challenge these children to write a paragraph using as many words from their spelling list as they can.

Homework / Additional activities

Spelling test

Ask the children to learn one of the following lists of words for a spelling test. Challenge them to write sentences for five of the words on their list.

Core words	Support words	Challenge words
mixture	mixture	mixture
departure	departure	departure
capture	capture	capture
adventure	adventure	adventure
nature	nature	nature
picture	picture	picture
future	future	future
creature	creature	creature
feature		feature
temperature		temperature
furniture		furniture
miniature		miniature
		vulture
		puncture
		moisture

Collins Connect: Unit 12

Ask the children to complete Unit 12 (See Teach → Year 3 → Spelling → Unit 12).

Unit 13: The ending –sion

Overview

English curriculum objectives

- Endings which sound like /zhun/

Treasure House resources

- Spelling Skills Pupil Book 3 Unit 13, pages 30–31
- Collins Connect Treasure House Spelling Year 3, Unit 13
- Photocopiable Unit 13 Resource 1: A spelling explo<u>sion</u>!, page 99

- Photocopiable Unit 13 Resource 2: A difficult deci<u>sion</u>: –tion or –<u>sion</u>?, page 100

Additional resources

- Word cards: vision, action, condition, division, station, television, explosion, nation, decision, confusion, condition, notion, information, occasion
- Slips of paper or card for making bookmarks

Introduction

Teaching overview

The buzzy /zhun/ sound at the ends of words such as 'television' and 'explosion' is usually spelt '–sion'. Children need to hear the difference between this ending and words such as 'station' and 'nation' that end with /shun/. Not all words ending '–sion' are pronounced /zhun/ (see Unit 15), but almost all words pronounced /zhun/ are spelt '–sion'.

Introduce the concept

Write the word 'information' on the board and remind the children about previous work on the '–tion'

and '–ation' endings. Read the word together and agree that the end sound is /shun/. Now write the word 'television' on the board and ask the children to read the word and compare its ending with that of 'information'. Help the children to hear the buzzy /zhun/ ending. Organise the children into groups and give each group a set of the word cards (see Additional resources). Ask them to read the words carefully (listening to each other) and sort them into words that end /zhun/ and words that end /shun/. Compare the findings and explain that when we hear the /zhun/ ending, the spelling is usually '–sion'.

Pupil practice

Pupil Book pages 30–31

Get started

The children copy words and underline the '–sion' endings. Read the words together and ensure the children can hear the /zhun/ sound.

Answers

1. *televi<u>sion</u>*		*[example]*
2. divi<u>sion</u>		[1 mark]
3. vi<u>sion</u>		[1 mark]
4. confu<u>sion</u>		[1 mark]
5. inva<u>sion</u>		[1 mark]
6. deci<u>sion</u>		[1 mark]
7. explo<u>sion</u>		[1 mark]
8. provi<u>sion</u>		[1 mark]

Try these

The children choose the correct spellings of words. Remind the children that they are practising the /zhun/ sound spelt '–sion'.

Answers

1. *illusion*	*[example]*
2. revision	[1 mark]
3. conclusion	[1 mark]
4. occasion	[1 mark]
5. collision	[1 mark]
6. version	[1 mark]

Now try these

The children compose sentences for target words 'division', 'illusion', 'conclusion', 'revision', 'collision' and 'invasion'.

Answers

1. *There was confusion over school opening times.* *[example]*

Accept sentences in which the target word is spelt correctly. [6 marks: 1 per sentence]

Support, embed & challenge

Support

As a group, read the word cards (see Additional resources) and ensure that all the children can hear the difference between the /zhun/ and the /shun/ endings.

Ask the children to complete Unit 13 Resource 1: A spelling explo<u>sion</u>! (**Answers** ending '–sion': vision, division, television, explosion, decision, confusion, occasion; ending '–tion': action, condition, station, nation, notion, information)

Ask the children to write '–tion' on one side of their whiteboards and '–sion' on the other. Read the words from the word cards and Unit 13 Resource 1: A spelling explo<u>sion</u>!, adding more words, such as 'operation', 'population', 'conclusion', 'occasion', 'invasion' and 'illusion'. Ask the children to hold up the appropriate spelling pattern for each word.

Embed

Ask the children to collate all the '–sion' words that they practised in the Pupil Book and starter activities and all the '–ation' words practised in Unit 9. Provide slips of paper or card and instruct the children to write all the '–tion' and '–sion' words on their slips, decorate them, and then use them as bookmarks for the week.

Ask the children to complete Unit 13 Resource 2: A difficult deci<u>sion</u>: –tion or –sion? (**Answers** 1. explosion, 2. decision, 3. actions, 4. confusion, 5. information, 6. television, 7. station, 8. condition)

Challenge

Ask these children to investigate the meanings of the words 'supervision', 'erosion', 'precision', 'diversion' and 'intrusion'.

Homework / Additional activities

Spelling test

Ask the children to learn one of the following lists of words for a spelling test. Challenge them to write sentences for five of the words on their list.

Core words	Support words	Challenge words
vision	vision	vision
division	division	division
television	television	television
explosion	explosion	explosion
decision	decision	decision
conclusion	conclusion	conclusion
confusion	confusion	confusion
occasion	occasion	occasion
invasion		invasion
illusion		illusion
		revision
		collision
		provision

Collins Connect: Unit 13

Ask the children to complete Unit 13 (See Teach → Year 3 → Spelling → Unit 13).

Unit 14: The suffix –ous

Overview

English curriculum objectives

- The suffix '–ous'

Treasure House resources

- Spelling Skills Pupil Book 3 Unit 14, pages 32–33
- Collins Connect Treasure House Spelling Year 3, Unit 14
- Photocopiable Unit 14 Resource 1: Advantage<u>ous</u> –ous words, page 101

- Photocopiable Unit 14 Resource 2: Spelling numer<u>ous</u> –ous words, page 102

Additional resources

- Word cards: furious, marvellous, anxious, glorious, dangerous, hazardous, disastrous, ridiculous, suspicious, poisonous, ambitious, numerous, glamorous, nervous, serious, various, curious, dangerous, enormous, fabulous, famous, furious, generous, mysterious, adventurous, mountainous, prosperous, famous

Introduction

Teaching overview

The rules for adding '–ous' to root words are truly dreadful! Here they are.

1. For many words, just add '–ous', for example, 'hazard' → 'hazardous'.
2. For words ending 'e', (usually) drop the 'e', for example, 'fame' → 'famous'.
3. For words with a soft /g/ ('ge'), keep the final 'e', for example, 'advantage' → 'advantageous'. There are very few of these words.
4. For words ending 'y', change the 'y' to an 'i', for example, 'glory' → 'glorious'.
5. For words ending 'our', change 'our' to 'or', for example, 'glamour' → 'glamorous'. There are not many of these words, either.
6. The '–ious' ending is more common than '–eous' but there are still quite a few words ending '–eous', such as 'gorgeous' and 'miscellaneous'.

7. Many words ending '–ous' have no clear root word, such as 'serious', 'obvious', 'curious' and 'enormous'.

Most of the words Year 3 children will want to spell will either end in just '–ous' or an easy-to-hear '–ious' so the focus at this time should be spelling the /us/ sound 'ous'.

Introduce the concept

Give each child a word card (see Additional resources). Ask the children to turn to a partner, read the word and decide if any part of it is difficult to spell. Tell them to join with another pair and discuss their four words. Ask each group to tell you their four words and what part of each word they find tricky to spell. Write the words on the board as they tell you them and underline the tricky parts. Ask: 'What sound do all these words end in? How is it spelt?'

Pupil practice

Pupil Book pages 32–33

Get started

The children copy words and underline the '–ous' endings. Afterwards, ask them to look at the root of the word (the part not underlined). Discuss whether the root is a word and whether it has been changed.

Answers

1. *raven<u>ous</u>*	*[example]*
2. poison<u>ous</u>	[1 mark]
3. fabul<u>ous</u>	[1 mark]
4. nerv<u>ous</u>	[1 mark]
5. ridicul<u>ous</u>	[1 mark]
6. hazard<u>ous</u>	[1 mark]

Try these

The children copy words and add 'ous' to the ends, changing the root words if necessary. Remind the children of the long list of rules about adding '–ous' to the end of a word.

Answers

1. *various*	*[example]*
2. courageous	[1 mark]

3. humorous [1 mark]

4. advantageous [1 mark]

5. prosperous [1 mark]

6. famous [1 mark]

7. adventurous [1 mark]

Now try these

The children compose sentences for the target words 'dangerous', 'glamorous', 'mountainous', 'hideous'

and 'nervous'. Ensure the children understand the meaning of each word before they write their sentences. Tell them to share their ideas with a partner first.

Answers

1. *Cats have a reputation for being curious. [example]*

Accept answers in which the target word has been spelt correctly. [5 marks: 1 per sentence]

Support, embed & challenge

Support

Focus with these children on creating a clear link in their minds between the /us/ sound and the '–ous' ending. Pull out the most useful and straightforward words and work with these, for example, 'famous', 'dangerous', 'serious', 'enormous' and 'generous'. Have the children practise reading these words from the word cards (see Additional resources), writing them out and underlining the /us/ sound for each one.

Ask the children to complete Unit 14 Resource 1: Advantage<u>ous</u> –ous words. (**Answers** 1. ridiculous, 2. poisonous, 3. nervous, 4. ravenous, 5. obvious, 6. hideous)

Embed

Ask the children to complete Unit 14 Resource 2: Spelling numer<u>ous</u> –ous words. (**Answers** ridiculous,

ambitious, glorious, hazardous, poisonous, furious, disastrous, glamorous, nervous, dangerous, anxious, suspicious, numerous, marvellous)

Once the children are confident with the words on Unit 14 Resource 2: Spelling numer<u>ous</u> –ous words, provide them with the corresponding word cards (see Additional resources) and copies of Unit 12 Resource 2: A spelling adven<u>ture</u> (page 98), along with a dice and counters. The children should play the game in groups of four.

Challenge

Ask these children to become confident spelling 'anxious', 'cautious', 'suspicious' and 'delicious'. Help them understand that, in these words, 'xi', 'ti' and 'ci' correspond to a /sh/ sound.

Homework / Additional activities

Spelling test

Ask the children to learn one of the following lists of words for a spelling test. Challenge them to write sentences for five of the words on their list.

Core words		Support words		Challenge words	
serious	furious	serious	fabulous	serious	generous
various	generous	various	famous	various	cautious
curious	cautious	curious	furious	curious	jealous
dangerous	jealous	dangerous	generous	dangerous	marvellous
enormous	marvellous	enormous		enormous	delicious
fabulous	delicious			fabulous	mysterious
famous				famous	disastrous
				furious	

Collins Connect: Unit 14

Ask the children to complete Unit 14 (See Teach → Year 3 → Spelling → Unit 14).

Unit 15: The endings –tion, –sion, –ssion and –cian

Overview

English curriculum objectives

* Endings which sound like /shun/ spelt '–tion', '–sion', '–ssion', '–cian'

Treasure House resources

* Spelling Skills Pupil Book 3 Unit 15, pages 34–35
* Collins Connect Treasure House Spelling Year 3, Unit 15
* Photocopiable Unit 15 Resource 1: Be a spelling magician, page 103
* Photocopiable Unit 15 Resource 2: An education in word extension, page 104

Additional resources

* Word cards: perfection, population, invention, mention, information, action, election, eruption, hesitation, education, information, question, direction, discussion, permission, percussion, expression, admission, confession, optician, magician, mathematician, musician, technician, expansion, extension, comprehension, tension, revulsion
* Adhesive putty to stick word cards to the board

Introduction

Teaching overview

The /shun/ sound is spelt '–tion', '–sion', '–ssion' and '–cian'. Of these, '–tion' is the most common. If the root word ends 't' or 'te', use '–tion' ('invent' → 'invention', 'hesitate' → 'hesitation'); if the root word ends 'ss' or 'mit', use '–ssion' ('discuss' → 'discussion', 'transmit' → 'transmission'); if the root word ends 'd' or 'se', use '–sion' ('expand' → 'expansion', 'tense' → 'tension'); if the root word ends 'c' or 'cs', use '–cian' ('music' → 'musician', 'mathematics' → 'mathematician'). Words with the '–cian' ending are mostly occupations, such as 'magician', 'physician', 'optician'.

Introduce the concept

Write the words 'discussion', 'musician', 'information' and 'tension' across the top of the board and read the words together. Underline the endings and make a connection to the '–ation' ending covered earlier. Give each child one of the word cards (see Additional resources). Ask them to have a go at reading their word, and the words of the children near them, helping each other as necessary. Tell them to underline the ending of the word on their card. Invite each child to come to the front and stick their word under the word on the board with the same ending. Together, deduce which ending is the most common ('–tion'). Ask: 'What do the words that end '–cian' have in common?' (They are occupations.)

Pupil practice

Pupil Book pages 34–35

Get started

The children copy words and then underline the spellings of the /shun/ sound. Afterwards, ask them to sort the words into the different spelling patterns.

Answers

1. discu<u>ssion</u>	[example]
2. musi<u>cian</u>	[1 mark]
3. percu<u>ssion</u>	[1 mark]
4. ac<u>tion</u>	[1 mark]
5. ten<u>sion</u>	[1 mark]
6. admi<u>ssion</u>	[1 mark]
7. elec<u>tion</u>	[1 mark]

Try these

The children look at three spelling options for each word and decide which is the correct spelling. Remind them that the original root word (if they know it) might give them a clue.

Answers

1. invention	[example]
2. politician	[1 mark]
3. injection	[1 mark]
4. magician	[1 mark]
5. eruption	[1 mark]
6. perfection	[1 mark]

Now try these

The children copy and complete the sentences by adding the correct suffix to the underlined words. Remind them that they might need to remove some letters from the root word. Ensure that the children understand the meaning of 'election' and 'obsession'.

Answers

1. *Rover the dog knew the direction home.* [example]

2. The Mayor worried about the coming election. [1 mark]

3. My sister is a very talented musician. [1 mark]

4. I can recite the alphabet without hesitation. [1 mark]

5. Football is Cynthia's growing obsession. [1 mark]

6. It is important to get a good education. [1 mark]

Support, embed & challenge

Support

Focus on the words ending '–tion' with these children. Place all the word cards that end '–tion' in the middle of the table (see Additional resources). Read the words together and check that the children understand them all. Next, say clues for each word, using the root word where possible. For example: 'Something an inventor invents is called an …' or 'What do we call an event held to elect our country's leaders?' Invite the children to find the word card with the word you describe. Discuss the composition of each word as it is covered. Once the children are confident with the words ending '–tion', repeat the process for words ending '–cian'.

Ask the children to complete Unit 15 Resource 1: Be a spelling magi**cian**. (**Answers** 1. beautician, 2. electrician, 3. magician, 4. musician, 5. technician, 6. mathematician, 7. politician, 8. optician)

Embed

Ask the children to complete Unit 15 Resource 2: An educa**tion** in word exten**sion**. (**Answers** possession, direction, depression, expression, hesitation, permission, extension, tension, election, eruption,

action, information, expansion, organisation, option, introduction, education) Ask the children about any patterns they found to help them spell the longer words. Hopefully, they will have noticed that the final letters of the root words give some indication as to which spelling of /shun/ should be used. For example, 'direct' and 'elect' take '–tion', as do 'hesitate' and 'educate'; 'possess', 'depress' and 'express' all take '–ssion'; 'extend' and 'expand' both take '–sion'. Afterwards, organise the children into pairs and tell the children to test each other using their completed sheets. Taking turns, one child in each pair should choose a root verb and say it to their partner. Their partner should then tell them the associated noun and try to spell it without looking at the sheet.

Challenge

Ask these children to investigate and study the rules for adding the /shun/ ending spelt '–tion', '–sion', '–ssion' or '–cian': use '–tion' for roots ending 't' or 'te', '–ssion' for roots ending 'ss' or 'mit'; '–sion' for roots ending 'd' or 'se'; '–cian' for roots ending 'c' or 'cs'. If they feel confident enough, encourage them to present the rules to the rest of the class.

Homework / Additional activities

Spelling test

Ask the children to learn one of the following lists of words for a spelling test. Challenge them to write sentences for five of the words on their list.

Core words		Support words		Challenge words	
relation	musician	relation	direction	relation	magician
solution	magician	solution	education	solution	expression
question	expression	station	information	direction	percussion
direction	session	action	musician	education	permission
education	permission	question	magician	position	possession
information	possession			eruption	expansion
position	tension			attention	tension
				musician	

Collins Connect: Unit 15

Ask the children to complete Unit 15 (See Teach → Year 3 → Spelling → Unit 15).

Unit 16: The /k/ sound spelt ch

Overview

English curriculum objectives
- Words with the /k/ sound spelt 'ch' (Greek in origin)

Treasure House resources
- Spelling Skills Pupil Book 3 Unit 16, pages 36–37

- Collins Connect Treasure House Spelling Year 3, Unit 16
- Photocopiable Unit 16 Resource 1: School bingo, page 105
- Photocopiable Unit 16 Resource 2: Improve your spelling technique, page 106

Introduction

Teaching overview
There are about 24 common words that spell the /k/ sound 'ch'. Of these, the most useful are: 'school', 'stomach', 'chorus', 'character', 'choir', 'scheme' and 'headache'.

Introduce the concept
Ask the children to suggest words with the /k/ sound, for example, 'kitten', 'back' or 'crumpet'. Write the words on the board and underline the letter or letters that represent the /k/ sound. Ask: 'How do you spell "school"?' Write the word on the board and ask a volunteer to underline the 'ch' spelling. Ask the children to help you spell 'stomach', 'chorus', 'character', 'choir', 'scheme', 'chaos', 'echo' and 'headache'. Hopefully they will pick up on the spelling pattern and begin to suggest it.

Pupil practice

Pupil Book pages 36–37

Get started
The children copy words and underline the 'ch' spelling of /k/ in each. Clarify the meanings of 'chorus', 'chord' and 'mechanic'.

Answers

1. *heada<u>ch</u>e*	*[example]*
2. <u>ch</u>emist	[1 mark]
3. <u>ch</u>orus	[1 mark]
4. s<u>ch</u>eme	[1 mark]
5. stoma<u>ch</u>	[1 mark]
6. s<u>ch</u>ool	[1 mark]
7. <u>ch</u>ord	[1 mark]
8. me<u>ch</u>anic	[1 mark]

Try these
The children copy sentences and underline the words in which the /k/ sound is spelt 'ch'. Warn them that each sentence also has a word in it where 'ch' represents /ch/.

Answers

1. *Tom's <u>stomach</u> hurt from eating too much cheese.*　　　　*[example]*

2. Cherries always give me tummy <u>ache</u>. [1 mark]

3. Charles called out and his voice made an <u>echo</u>. [1 mark]

4. The <u>school</u> rabbit was munching a carrot. [1 mark]

5. The room was in <u>chaos</u>, but Gran still looked cheery. [1 mark]

Now try these
The children copy and complete the sentences by choosing the correct spelling of the missing words. Warn the children that the activity contains words where the /k/ sound is spelt 'k' and words where /k/ is spelt 'ch'.

Answers

1. *Nina was looking forward to the school disco.*　　　　*[example]*

2. We went to the market with my aunt. [1 mark]

3. Flavia plays the saxophone in our town orchestra. [1 mark]

4. The kind old lady had made a cake. [1 mark]

5. We made the kitchen such a mess! [1 mark]

Support, embed & challenge

Support

Use Unit 16 Resource 1: School bingo to play 'Bingo' with these children. Play a few times so that the children cross off the letters of most, if not all, of the words. Afterwards, read the words one at a time and challenge the children to remember the spellings.

Embed

Ask the children to complete Unit 16 Resource 2: Improve your spelling technique. (**Answers** 1. anchor, 2. chaos, 3. choir, 4. echoed, 5. school, 6. headache, 7. stomach, 8. chorus)

Ask the children to write 'ch' on one side of their whiteboards and 'k' on the other. Read out the following words and ask the children to hold up 'ch' or 'k': 'kitchen', 'chaos', 'school', 'scooter', 'echo', 'bake', 'anchor', 'keep', 'chorus', 'steak', 'headache', 'stomach', 'kit', 'chasm', 'kick'. Read the words again and, this time, challenge the children to spell each word, writing it on their whiteboards each time.

Challenge

Ask these children to find out the meanings of the words 'orchid', 'monarch', 'chemist', and 'technical'.

Homework / Additional activities

Spelling test

Ask the children to learn one of the following lists of words for a spelling test. Challenge them to write sentences for five of the words on their list.

Core words	Support words	Challenge words
anchor	ache	anchor
chaos	anchor	chaos
choir	chaos	choir
chorus	choir	chorus
echo	chorus	echo
scheme	echo	scheme
school	scheme	school
headache	school	headache
character		character
mechanic		mechanic
		technical
		technology
		chasm

Collins Connect: Unit 16

Ask the children to complete Unit 16 (See Teach → Year 3 → Spelling → Unit 16).

Unit 17: The /sh/ sound spelt ch

Overview

English curriculum objectives
- Words with the /sh/ sound spelt 'ch' (mostly French in origin)

Treasure House resources
- Spelling Skills Pupil Book 3 Unit 17, pages 38–39
- Collins Connect Treasure House Spelling Year 3, Unit 17

- Photocopiable Unit 17 Resource 1: Be a spelling machine!, page 107
- Photocopiable Unit 17 Resource 2: Lunch at the chalet, page 108

Additional resources
- Word cards: machine, chef, quiche, chalet, brochure, chandelier, parachute, charade, machete, sachet

Introduction

Teaching overview
Although children need to be aware of the /sh/ sound spelt 'ch', most of the words with this spelling are not very useful for Year 3 children, with the exceptions of 'machine', 'chef' and, perhaps, 'moustache'. The names 'Michelle' and 'Charlotte' might be useful if the children know anyone by these names. Other words that can be used to practise this spelling are 'quiche', 'chalet', 'brochure', 'chandelier', 'parachute', 'charade', 'machete' and 'sachet'.

Introduce the concept
Ask the children to write a word with the /sh/ sound on their whiteboard and hold it up. Ask the children to look around the classroom and read the words. Discuss the 'sh' spelling for /sh/. Remind the children about the 'ch' spelling for the /k/ sound and recap on the words from Unit 16. Write 'motion', 'sure', 'chef' and 'machine' on the board and read them together, discussing which letters in each represent /sh/. Write 'quiche', 'chalet', 'brochure', 'chandelier', 'parachute', 'charade', 'machete', and 'sachet' on the board and ask volunteers to come out and underline the /sh/ sound in each word. (You might also want to point out the /k/ spelt 'qu' in 'quiche' and /ay/ spelt 'et' in 'chalet' and 'sachet' and the /ee/ spelt 'e' at the end of 'machete'.) Explain to the children that they should only spell /sh/ 'ch' when they know that it is the right spelling because it's not very common.

Pupil practice

Pupil Book pages 38–39

Get started
The children sort words into two spelling patterns: /sh/ spelt 'ch' and /sh/ spelt 'sh'. Afterwards, discuss other parts of 'moustache', 'machine' and 'chalet' that might cause spelling problems.

Answers

/sh/ spelt 'ch'		/sh/ spelt 'sh'	
moustache	[example]	ship	[1 mark]
chef	[1 mark]	fashion	[1 mark]
machine	[1 mark]	dish	[1 mark]
chalet	[1 mark]		
brochure	[1 mark]		

Try these
The children to use 'ch' or 'sh' to complete words. Afterwards, check the children know the meanings of 'chandelier', 'cashier', 'quiche' and 'sachet'.

Answers
1. chandelier   *[example]*
2. cashier   [1 mark]
3. quiche   [1 mark]
4. ashamed   [1 mark]
5. sachet   [1 mark]
6. cushion   [1 mark]

Now try these
The children choose the correct spelling for the missing word in each sentence and write the complete sentences.

Answers
1. *The parachutist floated safely to the ground. [example]*
2. I don't really care about following fashion. [1 mark]
3. The meal was cooked by an excellent chef. [1 mark]
4. I like a mushroom topping on my pizza. [1 mark]
5. I have a shower every day. [1 mark]

Support, embed & challenge

Support

Use the word cards (see Additional resources) to recap on the words from the Pupil Book activities: 'machine', 'chef', 'quiche', 'chalet', 'brochure', 'chandelier', 'parachute' and 'sachet'. Have the children practise reading these words from the word cards, writing them out and underlining the /sh/ sound.

Provide the children with Unit 17 Resource 1: Be a spelling machine! Ask the children to read each word and then colour in the words with the /sh/ sound spelt 'ch'. (**Answers** colour: chef, machete, quiche, machine, sachet, moustache, charade, parachute, chalet, brochure)

Work with the children in a group with a fresh copy of Unit 17 Resource 1: Be a spelling machine! Cut out the words and together sort them into /sh/ spelt 'sh', /sh/ spelt 'ch' and /ch/ spelt 'ch'.

Embed

Ask the children to complete Unit 17 Resource 2: Lunch at the chalet. (**Answers** in order: chalet, parachuted, machete, machine, chef, quiche, sachet, pistachios, brochures)

Have the children write 'sh' on one side of their whiteboards and 'ch' on the other. Read out the /sh/ words 'chef', 'machete', 'quiche', 'machine', 'sachet', 'moustache', 'charade', 'parachute', 'chalet', 'brochure'. For each word, ask the children to hold up the letters 'sh' or 'ch' on their whiteboards according to how they think the /sh/ sound is spelt.

Challenge

Provide these children with dictionaries. Ask them to investigate the meanings of the words 'chic' and 'chandelier', writing a sentence for each.

Encourage them to investigate the origins of some of the /sh/ spelt 'ch' words they have learned to see if they can find a pattern. (All the words are French in origin except 'machete', which is Spanish.)

Homework / Additional activities

Spelling test

Ask the children to learn one of the following lists of words for a spelling test. Challenge them to write sentences for five of the words on their list.

Core words	Support words	Challenge words
moustache	chef	moustache
chef	moustache	chef
machine	machine	machine
parachute	parachute	parachute
charade	charade	charade
machete	machete	machete
quiche	quiche	quiche
sachet	sachet	sachet
chalet	chalet	chalet
brochure	brochure	brochure
		chandelier
		chic

Collins Connect: Unit 17

Ask the children to complete Unit 17 (See Teach → Year 3 → Spelling → Unit 17).

Review unit 2

A. Ask children to write down the correct spelling of each word.

1. measure [1 mark]
2. pleasure [1 mark]
3. adventure [1 mark]
4. creature [1 mark]
5. future [1 mark]
6. nature [1 mark]
7. television [1 mark]
8. nervous [1 mark]
9. discussion [1 mark]
10. headache [1 mark]
11. stomach [1 mark]
12. machine [1 mark]

B. Ask children to add the suffixes to the words. Remind the children that they might need to change the ending of the word before they add the suffix.

1. exploration [1 mark]
2. inspiration [1 mark]
3. preparation [1 mark]
4. busily [1 mark]
5. happily [1 mark]
6. noisily [1 mark]

C. Ask the children to write the sentences and complete the missing word in each sentence.

1. The pirates used a map to find the treasure buried on the island. [1 mark]
2. Joe painted a picture of his granny. [1 mark]
3. Toni had a very difficult decision to make: strawberry or chocolate ice cream. [1 mark]
4. In all the confusion at the end of the party, Suzy forgot her coat. [1 mark]
5. The invention of the internet has changed our lives. [1 mark]
6. Mrs Mason's hat was so ridiculous, we couldn't stop laughing. [1 mark]
7. The musicians playing in the market square cheered us up. [1 mark]
8. We all joined in with the chorus of the song. [1 mark]
9. I love cooking. I want to be a chef when I grow up. [1 mark]
10. The glamorous film star walked down the red carpet. [1 mark]

Unit 18: The sound /k/ spelt –que and the sound /g/ spelt –gue

Overview

English curriculum objectives
- Words ending with the /g/ sound spelt '–gue' and the /k/ sound spelt '–que' (French in origin)

Treasure House resources
- Spelling Skills Pupil Book 3 Unit 18, pages 42–43
- Collins Connect Treasure House Spelling Year 3, Unit 18

- Photocopiable Unit 18 Resource 1: A unique challenge, page 109
- Photocopiable Unit 18 Resource 2: A catalogue of –que and –gue words, page 110

Additional resources
- Word cards: tongue, rogue, league, meringue, catalogue, vague, antique, conquered, cheque, unique, grotesque, technique

Introduction

Teaching overview

The /g/ sound at the ends of a few words is spelt '–gue', for example, 'league', 'tongue', 'rogue', 'vague', 'meringue' and 'catalogue'. The /k/ sound at the ends of a few words is spelt '–que', for example, 'antique', 'cheque', 'unique' and 'grotesque'. Words such as 'queue', 'conquer' and 'chequered' also have the 'que' for /k/ spelling pattern, but at the beginning or in the middle of the words. The words with these spelling patterns tend not to be very useful for Year 3 children. However, they do need to be aware of the spelling patterns.

Introduce the concept

Ask the children to suggest words with the /k/ sound, for example, 'kitten', 'back' or 'crumpet'. Hopefully, the children will also suggest words with the /k/ sound spelt 'ch', such as 'stomach', 'chorus' or 'character'. Write the words the children suggest on the board and underline the letter or letters that represent the /k/ sound. Ask: 'Does anybody know how to spell "antique"?' Take suggestions, then write the word on the board and ask a volunteer to

underline the 'que' spelling. Ask the children to help you spell 'plaque', 'cheque', 'unique' and 'grotesque'. Hopefully they will pick up on the spelling pattern and begin to suggest it. Ensure the children understand the meaning of each word. Clarify the difference between the words 'check' (inspect) and 'cheque' (an order to a bank to pay money). Write the word 'technique' on the board. Ensure the children recognise and understand it. Point out that there are two spellings of /k/ in this word and ask a volunteer to find and underline them both.

Write the word 'rogue' on the board and ask the children to help you read it. Underline the 'gue' spelling of /g/ and explain that there are a few words with this spelling that they are going to learn. Write the words 'tongue', 'league', 'meringue', 'catalogue' and 'vague' on the board and ask volunteers to read them out. Discuss the meaning of each word. Ask the children to write the two words they think will be most useful in their writing. Give them a few minutes to memorise the words then ask the children to get into pairs and test each other on spelling their chosen words.

Pupil practice

Pupil Book pages 42–43

Get started

The children sort words into two groups: words where /k/ is spelt '–que' and words where /g/ is spelt '–gue'. Before they do so, read the words with the children, asking any ballerinas to explain what an 'arabesque' is (if they know). Explain the meaning of 'boutique' and 'rogue'. When the children are confident reading the words, ask them to sort them into the two spelling patterns.

Answers

/k/ spelt '–que'		/g/ spelt '–gue'	
arabesque	[example]	tongue	[1 mark]
antique	[1 mark]	rogue	[1 mark]
cheque	[1 mark]	league	[1 mark]
boutique	[1 mark]	meringue	[1 mark]

Try these

The children copy and complete words by adding '–que' or '–gue'. Before they do so, look at the activity with the children, telling them what the word is in each instance. When they are confident in the words they are spelling, ask them to choose the '–que' or '–gue' spelling.

Answers

1. *tongue*	*[example]*
2. league	[1 mark]
3. antique	[1 mark]
4. rogue	[1 mark]
5. boutique	[1 mark]

Now try these

The children copy and complete sentences by choosing the correct spellings of the missing words.

Before they do so, read the sentences with the children. Read the different spelling options together asking the children to sound out each, remembering the pronunciation of '–que' and '–gue'. Ask: 'Which sounds like a word you know?' Discuss the meaning of 'conquered', 'plague' and 'plaque'. When the children are confident about the vocabulary, ask them to complete the activity.

Answers

1. *The film about sharks contained very little dialogue.*	*[example]*
2. The Normans conquered England in 1066.	[1 mark]
3. The millionaire signed a large cheque.	[1 mark]
4. The Great Plague was also known as the Black Death.	[1 mark]
5. We had to queue for ages at the supermarket.	[1 mark]

Support, embed & challenge

Support

Focus with these children on reading and understanding the words by asking the children to complete Unit 18 Resource 1: A unique challenge. Afterwards, read all the words together sounding out the phonemes and clarifying the meanings. (**Answers** example word path (but others are possible): plaque, kite, antique, scabs, cold, crumble, mosque, snakes, cheque, chequers, king, arabesque)

Embed

Ask the children to complete Unit 18 Resource 2: A catalogue of –que and –gue words. (**Answers** 1. tongue, 2. Rogue, 3. belong, 4. League,

5. catalogue; 1. trek, 2. unique, 3. Greek, 4. technique, 5. grotesque)

Organise the children into pairs. Provide them with the word cards (see Additional resources) and ask them to sort them to into '–que' or '–gue' endings. Once they have sorted the cards, challenge the pairs to use one of the sets to play a memory game: Player 1 looks at all the cards. The cards are muddled and player 2 takes one away. Player 1 must guess which card has been taken away.

Challenge

Many of the words in this unit are tricky for Year 3 children. Challenge these children to compose sentences for any of the words covered in this unit.

Homework / Additional activities

Spelling test

Ask the children to learn one of the following lists of words for a spelling test. Challenge them to write sentences for five of the words on their list.

Core words		Support words		Challenge words	
tongue	antique	tongue	vague	tongue	antique
rogue	conquered	rogue	antique	rogue	conquered
league	unique	league	unique	league	cheque
catalogue	grotesque			meringue	unique
vague	technique			catalogue	grotesque
				vague	technique

Collins Connect: Unit 18

Ask the children to complete Unit 18 (See Teach → Year 3 → Spelling → Unit 18).

Unit 19: The sound /s/ spelt sc

Overview

English curriculum objectives

- Words with the /s/ sound spelt 'sc' (Latin in origin)

Treasure House resources

- Spelling Skills Pupil Book 3 Unit 19, pages 44–45
- Collins Connect Treasure House Spelling Year 3, Unit 19

- Photocopiable Unit 19 Resource 1: Searching for scissors, page 111
- Photocopiable Unit 19 Resource 2: Spelling with sc, page 112

Additional resources

- Blank cards for making word cards with the children

Introduction

Teaching overview

The /s/ sound is spelt 'sc' in a few words, including 'scene', 'scent', 'science', 'scissors', 'crescent', 'descend', 'science', 'muscles'. The most useful of these words is 'scissors'.

Introduce the concept

Write the words 'scene', 'birds', 'poster', 'seen', 'scent', 'science', 'whisper', 'scissors', 'lace', 'city', 'crescent', 'same', 'descend', 'cinema', 'bicycle', 'muscles', 'sing' and 'close' on the board in any order. Read the words together and locate the /s/ sound in each. Write 'sc', 'c' and 's' as headings across the top of the board and ask volunteers to come to the front and sort the words. Read through the words with the 'sc' spelling pattern together. Clarify the difference in the meanings of the words 'scene' (a location) and 'seen' (the past participle of 'see').

Pupil practice

Pupil Book pages 44–45

Get started

The children sort words into two groups: /s/ spelt 'sc' and /s/ spelt 's' or 'c'. Read the words together, clarifying their meanings, in particular 'scent', 'sent', 'descent', 'decent' and 'crescent'.

Answers

/s/ spelt 'sc'		/s/ spelt 's' or 'c'	
descend	[1 mark]	song	[example]
scene	[1 mark]	decent	[1 mark]
scent	[1 mark]	seen	[1 mark]
crescent	[1 mark]	sent	[1 mark]

Try these

The children write words and underline the 'sc' spelling. Emphasise the relationship between the spelling and pronunciation.

Answers

1. scissors	[example]
2. descend	[1 mark]
3. abscess	[1 mark]
4. scent	[1 mark]
5. scenery	[1 mark]
6. fascinate	[1 mark]

Now try these

The children compose sentences for the target words 'muscles', 'crescent', 'scent' and 'science'. Clarify the meanings of 'scenic' and 'scent' before asking the children to write a sentence for each word.

Answers

1. *Helen and Andrew walked a scenic route.* [example]

Accept answers in which the target words are spelt correctly. [4 marks: 1 per sentence]

Support, embed & challenge

Support

Ask the children to help you make word cards for the words 'scene', 'scent', 'science', 'scissors', 'crescent', 'descend' and 'muscles', illustrating them where possible.

Ask the children to complete the word search on Unit 19 Resource 1: Searching for <u>sc</u>issors. **Answers**

a	g	c	r	e	s	c	e	n	t	v
s	s	c	h	s	c	e	n	t	j	k
c	a	r	f	h	s	v	e	n	t	b
e	f	b	d	h	g	p	m	x	j	f
n	s	v	e	n	t	q	u	n	q	t
e	d	k	s	c	i	s	s	o	r	s
x	n	d	c	a	w	g	c	k	v	p
s	c	i	e	n	c	e	l	w	x	j
t	j	v	n	x	t	w	e	v	d	g
b	n	q	d	h	p	h	s	k	a	f
s	c	v	g	t	d	c	s	g	d	h

Embed

Provide the children with the words from the bottom of Unit 19 Resource 2: Spelling with <u>sc</u> – 'scissors', 'science', 'crescent', 'descend', 'scene', 'muscles' and 'scent'. Ask them to write the words down, then think of other words with the /s/ sound, such as 'stove', 'sling' or 'scooter', and write those words down too. Tell the children to read their words to a partner and test whether their partner can say if the /s/ sound is spelt 's' or 'sc' in each word.

Ask the children to complete Unit 19 Resource 2: Spelling with <u>sc</u>. (**Answers** 1. scene, 2. scent, 3. science, 4. scissors, 5. crescent, 6. descent, 7. muscles)

Challenge

Ask these children to research and learn the meanings of the homophones and near homophones 'scent' and 'sent', 'decent' and 'descent', 'seen' and 'scene', 'muscles' and 'mussels'.

Homework / Additional activities

Spelling test

Ask the children to learn one of the following lists of words for a spelling test. Challenge them to write sentences for five of the words on their list.

Core words	Support words	Challenge words
scene	scene	scene
scent	scent	scent
science	science	science
scissors	scissors	scissors
crescent	crescent	crescent
descend	descend	descend
science		science
muscles		muscles
		fascinate
		scenery

Collins Connect: Unit 19

Ask the children to complete Unit 19 (See Teach → Year 3 → Spelling → Unit 19).

Unit 20: The sound /ay/ spelt ei, eigh and ey

Overview

English curriculum objectives
- Words with the /ay/ sound spelt 'ei', 'eigh', or 'ey'

Treasure House resources
- Spelling Skills Pupil Book 3 Unit 20, pages 46–47
- Collins Connect Treasure House Spelling Year 3, Unit 20

- Photocopiable Unit 20 Resource 1: The aim of the game: Find words that sound the same, page 113
- Photocopiable Unit 20 Resource 2: ei, eigh and ey crossword, page 114

Additional resources
- Word cards: sleigh, weigh, weight, eight, eighteen, neighbour, beige, they, grey, obey, prey, reindeer

Introduction

Teaching overview
The long /ay/ sound can be spelt 'ei' as in 'vein', 'rein' and 'veil'; 'eigh' as in eight, 'weight' and 'neighbour'; 'ey' as in 'grey', 'prey' and 'obey'.

Introduce the concept
Recap on the spellings of the long /ay/ sound that the children should already know. Ask the children to write one word on their whiteboard with the long /ay/ sound in it and then hold it up. Pick out words with different spellings and write them on the board, for example 'train', 'plate' and 'play'. Write the words 'sleigh', 'weigh', 'weight', 'eight', 'eighteen', 'neighbour', 'beige', 'they', 'grey', 'obey', 'prey' and 'reindeer' on the board. Read the words together, clarifying meanings where necessary, and ask volunteers to underline the long /ay/ sound in each. Sort the words into the different spelling patterns. Explain that there are not many words with /ay/ spelt 'ei', 'eigh' and 'ey', but that some of them are quite useful. Remind the children that these are uncommon spellings so they should learn them for these words, but continue to use 'ay', 'ai', or 'a_e' as their best bet if they are unsure.

Pupil practice

Pupil Book pages 46–47

Get started
The children sort words into three groups: /ay/ spelt 'ei', /ay/ spelt 'eigh' and /ay/ spelt 'ey'. Before they do so, read the words together.

Answers

/ay/ spelt 'ei'	/ay/ spelt 'eigh'		/ay/ spelt 'ey'	
beige [example]	eighteen	[1 mark]	convey	[1 mark]
	weightlifter	[1 mark]	survey	[1 mark]
	neighbourhood	[1 mark]	prey	[1 mark]
	paperweight	[1 mark]		

Try these
The children copy words and underline the letters that represent the /ay/ sound. Before they do so, read the words together.

Answers
1. e<u>igh</u>t   *[example]*
2. ob<u>ey</u>   [1 mark]
3. sl<u>eigh</u>   [1 mark]
4. v<u>ei</u>l   [1 mark]
5. <u>eigh</u>ty   [1 mark]

Now try these
The children copy and complete sentences by choosing the correct spellings of the missing words. Before they do so, read the sentences together and clarify the missing words.

Answers

1. *The lion stalks its prey.* [example]
2. Hamid's alarm clock rang at eight o'clock. [1 mark]

3. The old man had a grey beard. [1 mark]
4. The King's reign lasted many years. [1 mark]
5. Blood runs through our veins. [1 mark]

Support, embed & challenge

Support

Read the word cards with these children (see Additional resources). Cut the word cards into phonemes and use them to practise segmenting and blending the words.

Ask the children to complete Unit 20 Resource 1: The aim of the game: Find words that sound the same. After the children have created a number of pairs, cut out all the words and make more pairs, ensuring that each pair has one word that follows this unit's spelling pattern. (**Answers** pairs of: prey, tray, grey, obey, delay, sleigh, play; pairs of: plate, weight, wait, straight, fate, ate, great, late, eight, rate; pairs of: train, plane, vein, rain, crane; veil, pail)

Embed

Ask the children to complete Unit 20 Resource 2: ei, eigh and ey crossword. (**Answers** 1. sleigh,

2. eighteen, 3. grey, 4. weight, 5. vein, 6. neighbour, 7. eight, 8. beige, 9. prey)

Tell the children to play 'Hangman' with a partner. Stipulate that every word they use for the game must have a long /ay/ sound in it.

Challenge

Challenge these children to come up with a list of as many words as they can with the spelling patterns 'ey', 'ei' or 'eigh' for the /ay/ sound. Tell them that a good way to expand their lists is to take a root word and then think of all the words that come from that root by adding prefixes, suffixes and creating compound words, for example, 'weigh' → 'weight', 'weighty', 'weightless', 'weighing', 'weighed', 'paperweight', 'weightlifter', 'counterweight'.

Homework / Additional activities

Spelling test

Ask the children to learn one of the following lists of words for a spelling test. Challenge them to write sentences for five of the words on their list.

Core words		Support words		Challenge words	
they	neighbour	they	neighbour	they	obey
sleigh	survey	sleigh	grey	sleigh	prey
weigh	grey	weight	obey	weigh	reindeer
weight	obey	eight	reindeer	weight	beige
eight	prey	eighteen		eight	rein
eighteen	reindeer			eighteen	veil
				neighbour	veins
				survey	convey
				grey	

Collins Connect: Unit 20

Ask the children to complete Unit 20 (See Teach → Year 3 → Spelling → Unit 20).

Unit 21: The possessive apostrophe with plural words

Overview

English curriculum objectives

• Possessive apostrophe with plural words

Treasure House resources

• Spelling Skills Pupil Book 3 Unit 21, pages 48–49
• Collins Connect Treasure House Spelling Year 3, Unit 21

• Photocopiable Unit 21 Resource 1: The nouns' apostrophes, page 115
• Photocopiable Unit 21 Resource 2: The apostrophes of the nouns, page 116

Introduction

Teaching overview

The correct placing of the possessive apostrophe can catch us all out at times. The rules are:

1. If the plural noun ends with an 's', then just add the apostrophe, as in 'the twins' party', 'the cherries' pips', 'the trees' roots'.

2. If the plural noun does not end with an 's' then add apostrophe + 's', as in 'the men's cheering', 'the people's princess'.

When trying to decide where to put the apostrophe, children must first establish whether the 's' at the end of a word denotes a plural, a possessive singular or a possessive plural.

Introduce the concept

Write the following sentences on the board and ask the children to help you decide which of them need an apostrophe: 'This weeks spellings are on the board.' 'The oranges are juicy.' 'The cows mooed in the barn.' 'We heard the mans footsteps in the corridor.' Agree that 'weeks' and 'mans' need apostrophes: 'This week's spellings', 'the man's footsteps'.

Change the first sentence to 'The next two weeks' spellings'. Change the fourth sentence to 'The men's footsteps'. Introduce the rule for adding the possessive apostrophe to plural nouns: if a plural noun ends 's', just add the apostrophe; if a plural noun doesn't end 's', add an apostrophe + 's'.

Pupil practice

Pupil Book pages 48–49

Get started

The children pair up singular and plural nouns. Afterwards, discuss the different spelling patterns.

Answers

1. girl————f) girls		[example]
2. cat————d) cats		[1 mark]
3. child————g) children		[1 mark]
4. lorry————e) lorries		[1 mark]
5. puppy————a) puppies		[1 mark]
6. chair————h) chairs		[1 mark]
7. man————b) men		[1 mark]
8. goose————c) geese		[1 mark]

Try these

The children write 'singular' or 'plural' to describe underlined words in sentences. Afterwards, ask the children to identify the object or objects being

possessed in each sentence ('toys', 'egg', 'food', 'coats', 'hairbands'). Ask: 'Which nouns still have an 's' at the end?'

Answers

1. *plural*	[example]
2. singular	[1 mark]
3. singular	[1 mark]
4. plural	[1 mark]
5. plural	[1 mark]

Now try these

The children copy and complete sentences by choosing the correct use of possessive apostrophes. Ask the children to discuss with a partner whether the missing nouns in the sentences should be singular or plural. Tell them that there are clues in each sentence to help them find out. Next, tell them to remember the rules for adding possessive apostrophes: Do they need to add an 's'? Where should the apostrophe go?

Answers

1. *Chloe held on tightly to the puppies' leads.* [example]

2. The books' covers were worn. [1 mark]

3. The women's boots were waterproof. [1 mark]

4. James's favourite drink was milkshake. [1 mark]

5. Khalid stayed at his friend's house. [1 mark]

Support, embed & challenge

Support

Ask the children to complete Unit 21 Resource 1: The nouns' apostrophes, which provides further practice in adding the possessive apostrophe to singular nouns and spotting singular and plural nouns in a possessive context. Afterwards, link their answers to the position of the apostrophes. (**Answers** 1. teacher's, 2. chair's, 3. dog's, 4. sister's, 5. Today's; 1. singular, 2. plural, 3. singular, 4. plural, 5. singular.

Read the following phrases and, for each phrase, ask the children to tell you whether they can hear a possessive noun: 'apples and pears', 'the cat's whiskers', 'a box of sweets', 'the lion's mane', 'the snake's tongue', 'the cows in the barn', 'Mr Mark's bike was stolen', 'the bikes were stolen'. Write the phrases out and invite the children to tell you where you need to put the apostrophes.

Work through Unit 21 Resource 2: The apostrophe of the nouns, as a group. (**Answers** *1. One week's holiday [example]*, 2. Two weeks' holiday, 3. Sam's hat, 4. The boys' hats, 5. The moon's light, 6. The stars' light, 7. The child's work, 8. The children's work, 9. The frog's eggs, 10. The frogs' eggs, 11. The tree's leaves, 12. The trees' leaves)

Embed

Ask the children to complete Unit 21 Resource 2: The apostrophe of the nouns. (**Answers** – see above)

Provide the children with sentences 1, 2 and 3 from Unit 21 Resource 1: The nouns' apostrophes, and ask them to make the nouns in each sentence plural, adjust the grammar accordingly and add the apostrophes in the correct places. Some children may need help with this task. (The sentences should read: 'The teachers' pens are on their desks.' 'The chairs' legs are wobbly.' 'Our dogs' barks are very loud.')

Challenge

Ask these children to write sentences about books belonging to children, the paws of some cats and the songs of the workmen.

Homework / Additional activities

Spelling test

Ask the children to learn one of the following lists of phrases for a test.

Core phrases	Support phrases	Challenge phrases
Sam's bike	Sam's bike	Sam's bike
the teacher's pen	the teacher's pen	the teacher's pen
the table's leg	the table's leg	the table's leg
Granny's house	Granny's house	Granny's house
the water's edge	my sister's friend	the water's edge
James's hat	the water's edge	James's hat
the year's end	the twins' party	the year's end
your heart's desire	all the boys' coats	your heart's desire
this week's spelling	the children's smiles	this week's spelling
next month's topic		next month's topic
in two months' time		in two months' time
the phone's battery		the phone's battery
the twins' party		the twins' party
all the boys' coats		all the boys' coats
		the boats' masts
		the cars' engines

Collins Connect: Unit 21

Ask the children to complete Unit 21 (See Teach → Year 3 → Spelling → Unit 21).

Unit 22: Homophones and near-homophones (1)

Overview

English curriculum objectives
- Homophones and near-homophones

Treasure House resources
- Spelling Skills Pupil Book 3 Unit 22, pages 50–51
- Collins Connect Treasure House Spelling Year 3, Unit 22
- Photocopiable Unit 22 Resource 1: Who's accepting a spelling medal?, page 117
- Photocopiable Unit 22 Resource 2: Effect versus affect, page 118

Additional resources
- Word cards: bury, berry, accept, except, medal, meddle, who's, whose, affect, effect, weather, whether
- Sentence cards: 'The dog will bury her bone.' 'The berry is red and juicy.' 'I accept the challenge!' 'Jane talks to everyone except me.' 'The officer won a medal for bravery.' 'Don't meddle with other people's lives.' 'Who's the tallest in the class?' 'Whose pencil case is this?' 'Your actions may affect others.' 'Wait an hour for the medicine to have an effect.' 'The weather is sunny and warm.' 'I can't decide whether to eat cake or jelly.'

Introduction

Teaching overview

This unit covers the homophones 'bury' (cover over), 'berry' (small fruit with no stone), 'accept' (consent to have or do), 'except' (other than, or not including), 'medal' (metal disc given as an award), 'meddle' (interfere where one shouldn't), 'who's' (contraction of 'who is' or 'who has'), 'whose' (belonging to), 'affect' (make a difference to), 'effect' (result or consequence), 'weather' (state of the atmosphere) and 'whether' (expressing choice). The trickiest of these is the difference between 'affect' and 'effect'. These words will be covered again in Years 5 and 6 so, at this stage, it's worth sticking to the simplest definition: 'affect' is a verb (for example, 'The weather affects my mood') and 'effect' is a noun (for example, 'We created a nice effect with fairy lights').

Introduce the concept

Write the words 'bury', 'berry', 'accept', 'except', 'medal', 'meddle', 'who's', 'whose', 'weather' and 'whether' on the board. Organise the children into groups and assign a word to each group for them to define or use in a sentence. Assign the more difficult words to higher ability groups. Allow the children time to confer and then ask each group to give you the definition of their assigned word or use their word in context. Award a mark for each correct definition or sentence. If a group gets stuck or has mistaken the meaning of their word, give them the correct definition and ask a volunteer from the group to use the word in context.

Write 'effect' and 'affect' on the board and spend time explaining the difference in meaning between the two words. Emphasise that 'affect' is a verb and 'effect' is a noun.

Pupil practice

Pupil Book pages 50–51

Get started

The children sort the words into homophone and near-homophone pairs. Tell them to turn to a partner and discuss the meaning of each word. Next, the children match some of the words to their definitions.

Answers

berry, bury	[example]
accept, except	[1 mark]
affect, effect	[1 mark]
weather, whether	[1 mark]
who's, whose	[1 mark]
medal, meddle	[1 mark]

1. berry: a small juicy fruit — [example]
2. who's: a contraction of the words 'who' and 'is' or 'has' — [1 mark]
3. whose: belonging to — [1 mark]
4. meddle: to interfere or tinker — [1 mark]
5. except: not including — [1 mark]
6. bury: put in a hole and cover with earth — [1 mark]

Try these

The children write words and then write a homophone or near-homophone for each word.

Answers

1. *medal, meddle*		*[example]*
2. except, accept		[1 mark]
3. who's, whose		[1 mark]
4. effect, affect		[1 mark]
5. bury, berry		[1 mark]

Now try these

The children copy and complete sentences by choosing the correct words to fill the gaps.

Afterwards, ask the children to tell you the meanings of the words they didn't use. Together, make up sentences for the unused words 'whether', 'excepted', 'berry', 'meddle' and 'bury'.

Answers

1. *The weather was good for the school trip.*	*[example]*
2. Samira accepted the party invitation.	[1 mark]
3. Squirrels love to bury nuts in the garden.	[1 mark]
4. Jack proudly showed off his swimming medal.	[1 mark]
5. I bought a cake with a berry on top.	[1 mark]

Support, embed & challenge

Support

Display the word cards and sentence cards (see Additional resources), muddled on the table in front of the children. Ask them to match the words to the sentences. Point out 'an' before 'effect' in the sentence 'Wait an hour for the medicine to have an effect.' Emphasise that 'effect' is a noun.

Ask the children to complete Unit 22 Resource 1: Who's accepting a spelling medal?; (**Answers** bury – put in a hole and cover, berry – small juicy fruit, accept – agree to something, except – not including, medal – metal disk on a ribbon, meddle – interfere or fiddle, who's – short for 'who is' or 'who has', whose – belonging to whom, weather – the climate (rain, snow, sunshine), whether – indication there is a choice)

Embed

Write the words 'bury', 'berry', 'accept', 'except', 'medal', 'meddle', 'who's', 'whose', 'weather' and 'whether' on the board. Put the word cards in a hat (see Additional resources). (You may choose not to include cards for 'effect' and 'affect'.) Ask a volunteer to pick out a card. Tell them to use the word in a sentence. Prompt them to check the sentence with you first and provide ideas if they struggle. Direct the volunteer to say their sentence to the class. Tell the children to identify the word that was used on the board, write it on their whiteboard and then hold it up. Repeat the process until every child has picked a word and thought of a sentence for the word. (The word cards can be returned to the hat after each go.)

Ask the children to complete Unit 22 Resource 2: Effect versus affect. (**Answers** 1. affected, 2. effect, 3. affect, 4. effect, 5. effects, 6. affect)

Challenge

Ask these children to compose sentences using the words 'effect', 'affect', 'accept' and 'except'.

Homework / Additional activities

Spelling test

Ask the children to learn the following sentences.

I'm going to bury this treasure.	I hope the weather today will be sunny.
There was one berry left – I ate it.	I don't know whether to laugh or cry.
I accept your apology.	The weather affected my mood.
Everyone line up, except Lucy.	The special effects were great.
Who's having a packed lunch today?	Don't meddle with that – it's not yours.
Whose is this jumper?	Nina won a gold medal at the swimming gala.

Collins Connect: Unit 22

Ask the children to complete Unit 22 (See Teach → Year 3 → Spelling → Unit 22).

Unit 23: Homophones and near-homophones (2)

Overview

English curriculum objectives
- Homophones and near-homophones

Treasure House resources
- Spelling Skills Pupil Book 3 Unit 23, pages 52–53
- Collins Connect Treasure House Spelling Year 3, Unit 23
- Photocopiable Unit 23 Resource 1: I've <u>heard</u> you're <u>great</u> at spelling!, page 119
- Photocopiable Unit 23 Resource 2: 'Knot' not 'not', page 120

Additional resources
- Word cards: hear, here, grate, great, not, knot, grown, groan, heel, heal, he'll
- Sentence cards: 'I hear with my ear'. 'Do you want to sit here or there?' 'Grate the cheese onto a plate.' 'Peas are great to eat!' 'I can feel a pain in my heel.' 'I hope this cut will heal really soon.' 'He'll come soon – I know he will.' 'I know how to tie knots.' 'Nina is not being nice.' 'Gosh you've grown – you grow too fast.' '"Our boat has sunk," we groan.'

Introduction

Teaching overview
This unit covers the homophones 'hear' (detect sound), 'here' (this place), 'grate' (shred with a grater), 'great' (big or wonderful), 'not' (used to form a negative), 'knot' (fastening of looped rope or string), 'grown' (past participle of 'grow'), 'groan' (inarticulate sound conveying pleasure or pain), 'heel' (back part of the foot), 'heal' (become healthy again) and 'he'll' (contraction of 'he will'). Most of these words are pretty straightforward, although some of the meanings of 'grate' might not be known to all children: 'to shred with a grater', 'to scrape', 'to annoy' and 'a frame for a fire'.

Introduce the concept
Write the words 'hear', 'here', 'grate', 'great', 'not', 'knot', 'grown', 'groan', 'heel', 'heal' and 'he'll' on the board. Organise the children into groups and assign a word to each group for them to define or use in a sentence. Assign the more difficult words to higher ability groups. Allow the children time to confer and then ask each group to give you the definition of their assigned word or use their word in context. Award a mark for each correct definition or sentence. If a group gets stuck or has mistaken the meaning of their word, give them the correct definition and ask a volunteer from the group to use the word in context.

Challenge the children to provide further definitions for 'grate'.

Pupil practice

Pupil Book pages 52–53

Get started
The children sort words into homophone pairs. Tell them to turn to a partner and discuss the meaning of each word. Ask the children to tell you a third homophone for 'heel' and 'heal' ('he'll'). Next, the children match words to their definitions.

Answers

heel, heal	*[example]*
grate, great	[1 mark]
grown, groan	[1 mark]
here, hear	[1 mark]
knot, not	[1 mark]
1. *heel: the back of the foot*	*[example]*
2. he'll: a contraction of the words 'he' and 'will'	[1 mark]

3. heal: to become healthy again	[1 mark]
4. grown: when something has become larger	[1 mark]
5. groan: a noise of pain or despair	[1 mark]

Try these
The children write words and then write a homophone or near-homophone for each word.

Answers

1. *great, grate*	*[example]*
2. grown, groan	[1 mark]
3. heel, heal, he'll	[1 mark]
4. knot, not	[1 mark]
5. hear, here	[1 mark]

Now try these

The children choose the correct words to complete sentences. Afterwards, ask the children to tell you the meanings of the words they didn't use. Together, make up sentences for the unused words 'here', 'grown', 'nots', 'heel', 'he'll' and 'heal'.

Answers

1. *Dogs can <u>hear</u> very high-pitched sounds. [example]*

2. Tessa let out a <u>groan</u> at the awful joke.   [1 mark]

3. The sailor was glad he could tie so many <u>knots</u>.   [1 mark]

4. The cut on Majid's finger would not <u>heal</u>.   [1 mark]

5. The new shoes hurt Sheila's <u>heel</u>.   [1 mark]

Support, embed & challenge

Support

Display the word cards and sentence cards. Ask the children to match the words to the sentences. Hide the sentences from view leaving the word cards displayed. Read out each sentence and have the children race to touch the corresponding word card. Display the sentences again. Ask the children to underline the letters in each sentence that will help them to remember which homophone to use.

Ask the children to complete Photocopiable Unit 23 Resource 1: I've <u>heard</u> you're <u>great</u> at spelling! (**Answers** hear – detect sound, here – this place, grate – shred or annoy, great – big or wonderful, not – used to form a negative, knot – fastening of looped rope, grown – become bigger (in the past), groan – emotional grunt, heel – back of the foot, heal – mend a wound, he'll – short for 'he will')

Embed

Write the words 'hear', 'here', 'grate', 'great', 'not', 'knot', 'grown', 'groan', 'heel', 'heal' and 'he'll' on the

board. Put the word cards in a hat (see Additional resources). Ask a volunteer to pick out a card. Tell them to use the word in a sentence. Prompt them to check the sentence with you first and provide ideas if they struggle. Direct the volunteer to say their sentence to the class. Tell the children to identify the word that was used on the board, write it on their whiteboard and then hold it up. Repeat the process until every child has picked a word and thought of a sentence for the word. (The word cards can be returned to the hat after each go.)

Ask the children to complete Unit 23 Resource 2: 'Knot' not 'not'. (**Answers** 1. he'll, 2. hear, 3. groan, 4. here, 5. not, 6. Grate, 7. great, 8. grown, 9. heal, 10. heel, 11. knot)

Challenge

Challenge these children to write two sentences, one using 'grate' meaning 'grill for a fire' and one using 'grate' meaning 'to annoy' or 'scratch'.

Homework / Additional activities

Spelling test

Ask the children to learn the following sentences.

I hear with my ear.	He'll come soon – I know he will.
Do you want to sit here or there?	I know how to tie knots.
Grate the cheese onto a plate.	Nina is not being nice.
Peas are great to eat!	Gosh you've grown – you grow too fast.
I can feel a pain in my heel.	"Our boat has sunk," we groan.
I hope this cut will heal really soon.	

Collins Connect: Unit 23

Ask the children to complete Unit 23 (See Teach → Year 3 → Spelling → Unit 23).

Unit 24: Homophones and near-homophones (3)

Overview

English curriculum objectives
- Homophones and near-homophones

Treasure House resources
- Spelling Skills Pupil Book 3 Unit 24, pages 54–55
- Collins Connect Treasure House Spelling Year 3, Unit 24
- Photocopiable Unit 24 Resource 1: <u>Meet</u> simple words with <u>plain</u> meanings, page 121
- Photocopiable Unit 24 Resource 2: Spellings not to be <u>missed</u>, page 122

Additional resources
- Word cards: mist, missed, mane, main, plane, plain, peace, piece, meet, meat, fair, fare
- Word cards from Unit 22: bury, berry, accept, except, medal, meddle, who's, whose, affect, effect, weather, whether
- Word cards from Unit 23: hear, here, grate, great, not, knot, grown, groan, heel, heal, he'll
- Definition cards: encounter, flesh to eat, light fog, failed to hit, obvious or basic, aircraft, most important, long head or neck hair, part or section, calm or quiet, ticket price, equal or just

Introduction

Teaching overview
This unit covers the homophones 'mist' (light fog), 'missed' (failed to hit), 'mane' (long hair on the head or neck of a mammal), 'main' (chief or foremost), 'plane' (airplane), 'plain' (undecorated or obvious), 'peace' (calm or quiet), 'piece' (bit of something), 'meet' (come into the presence of), 'meat' (flesh as food), 'fair' (equal or just) and 'fare' (cost of a ticket to travel).

Introduce the concept
Give each child one of the word cards (see Additional resources), taking one yourself if you have an odd number of children. (Provide more able children with the trickier words, such as 'effect' and 'affect'.) Tell the children to search the room trying to find the other word that sounds like theirs. Explain that there will be one trio ('he'll', 'heel' and 'heal'). Tell them to discuss the meanings of the two (or three) words with their partner (or trio), then help each other to practise spelling the words. Encourage them to ask for help if they need the meanings of their words clarified. Ask the children with this unit's target words to come to the front in pairs and introduce their words.

Pupil practice

Pupil Book pages 54–55

Get started
The children sort words into homophones pairs. Tell them to turn to a partner and discuss the meaning of each word. Next, the children match some words to their definitions.

Answers

meet, meat	*[example]*
mist, missed	[1 mark]
plain, plane	[1 mark]
main, mane	[1 mark]
piece, peace	[1 mark]
fare, fair	[1 mark]

1. *mane: long hair on a horse's or lion's neck*   *[example]*
2. plane: a wide, flat, level surface   [1 mark]
3. plain: simple, basic or without decoration   [1 mark]
4. mist: tiny drops of water in the air   [1 mark]
5. piece: a part of something   [1 mark]
6. fare: the amount you pay to travel on a train   [1 mark]
7. meat: the flesh of animals   [1 mark]
8. peace: a state of calm or quiet   [1 mark]

Try these

The children identify and list the correctly spelt words in each set.

Answers

1. *plain, plane*		*[example]*
2. peace		[1 mark]
3. missed, mist		[2 marks]
4. meet		[1 mark]
5. piece		[1 mark]
6. fare, fair		[2 marks]

Now try these

The children copy sentences, choosing the correct word to complete each sentence. Afterwards, ask the children to tell you the meanings of the words they didn't use. Together, make up a sentence for the unused words 'main', 'missed', 'plane', 'peace' and 'fare'.

Answers

1. *The horse's <u>mane</u> was brushed for the show.*	*[example]*
2. The damp <u>mist</u> rose from the river.	[1 mark]
3. The wind swept across the grassy <u>plain</u>.	[1 mark]
4. Jamil found the last <u>piece</u> of the jigsaw.	[1 mark]
5. I went on all the scary rides at the <u>fair</u>.	[1 mark]

Support, embed & challenge

Support

Work with these children on recognising the different words: 'mist', 'missed', 'mane', 'main', 'plane', 'plain', 'peace', 'piece', 'meet', 'meat', 'fair' and 'fare'. Recap the meaning of each word, then place the word cards (see Additional resources) face down in a pile in the centre of the group. Ask the children to take turns to pick up a card and read it. Challenge the children to say what the word means, using the word in a sentence if they prefer. If they can say the meaning of the word, they get to keep the card.

Ask the children to complete Unit 24 Resource 1: <u>Meet</u> simple words with <u>plain</u> meanings. (**Answers** meet – come into the presence of, meat – flesh for eating, mist – light fog, missed – failed to catch or hit, plain – obvious or basic, plane – flying machine, main – most important, mane – long hair on an animal's head, piece – part of something, peace – calm, quiet or stillness, fare – cost of a ticket to travel, fair – equal and just)

Embed

Organise the children into pairs and give each pair a set of word cards and definition cards (see Additional resources). This game works best if both sets of cards look identical when placed face down. Tell the children to use the cards to play a game of 'Pairs', pairing the words and their meanings.

Ask the children to complete Unit 24 Resource 2: Spellings not to be <u>missed</u>. (**Answers** 1. meet, 2. missed, 3. plane, 4. main, 5. meat, 6. fair, 7. peace, 8. plain)

Challenge

Challenge these children to write sentences for the words 'missed' meaning 'felt sad to be apart from', 'plane' meaning 'flat surface', 'fare' meaning 'food', and/or 'fair' meaning 'light in colour' (referring to hair).

Homework / Additional activities

Spelling test

Ask the children to learn the following sentences.

A light mist hung in the air.	With the baby asleep, we had peace at last.
We ran fast but we missed the bus.	Do you want a piece of apple pie?
Zebras' manes are stripy like their bodies.	Let's go and meet Mummy from the train.
We drove along the main road into town.	A carnivore only eats meat.
The plane took off from the runway.	That's not fair!
I chose a bun with plain white icing.	Amir paid the bus fare and sat down.

Collins Connect: Unit 24

Ask the children to complete Unit 24 (See Teach → Year 3 → Spelling → Unit 24).

Unit 25: Homophones and near-homophones (4)

Overview

English curriculum objectives
- Homophones and near-homophones

Treasure House resources
- Spelling Skills Pupil Book 3 Unit 25, pages 56–57
- Collins Connect Treasure House Spelling Year 3, Unit 25
- Photocopiable Unit 25 Resource 1: Have you seen these spellings?, page 123
- Photocopiable Unit 25 Resource 2: Spellings to make or break you, page 124

Additional resources
- Word cards: ball, bawl, male, mail, brake, break, rain, rein, reign, seen, scene
- Word cards from Unit 23: hear, here, grate, great, not, knot, grown, groan, heel, heal, he'll
- Word cards from Unit 24: mist, missed, mane, main, plane, plain, peace, piece, meet, meat, fair, fare
- Definition cards: fancy party, cry or shout, a gender, delivered letters, slow down, fall apart, water droplets, guide strap, rule, see (in the past), part of a play

Introduction

Teaching overview
This unit covers the homophones 'ball' (sphere), 'bawl' (cry loudly), 'male' (gender), 'mail' (post), 'brake' (mechanically slow down a vehicle), 'break' (come apart), 'rain' (precipitation), 'rein' (guide straps), 'reign' (rule), 'seen' (past participle of 'see') and 'scene' (location or section of a play). Some children might not be familiar with the meaning of 'bawl' (to cry hard), 'rein' (straps used to guide beasts) or 'reign' (hold royal office).

Introduce the concept
Give each child one of the word cards (see Additional resources). Provide more able children with the trickier words. Ask the children to search the room to find the word (or words) that sound the same as the one they have. Inform them that there will be two trios: 'he'll', 'heel' and 'heal'; 'rain', 'rein' and 'reign'. Tell them to discuss the meanings of the two (or three) words with their partner (or trio) and then help each other to practise spelling their words. Encourage them to ask for help if they need the meanings of their words clarified. Ask the children with this unit's target words ('ball', 'bawl', 'male', 'mail', 'brake', 'break', 'rain', 'rein', 'reign', 'seen' and 'scene') to come to the front in pairs and introduce their words. Point out the spelling patterns 'ei' for /ay/ and 'sc' for /s/.

Pupil practice

Pupil Book pages 56–57

Get started
The children sort words into homophones pairs. Tell them to turn to a partner and discuss the meaning of each word. Then, the children match some words to their definitions.

Answers

male, mail	*[example]*
ball, bawl	[1 mark]
brake, break	[1 mark]
scene, seen	[1 mark]
rain, rein	[1 mark]
1. *mail: letters and parcels*	*[example]*
2. rain: water falling from the sky	[1 mark]
3. rein: a strap for guiding horses	[1 mark]
4. bawl: to cry loudly	[1 mark]

Try these
The children write words and then write a homophone or near-homophone for each word.

Answers

1. *rain, rein*   *[example]*

2. ball, bawl   [1 mark]

3. seen, scene   [1 mark]

4. scene, seen   [1 mark]

5. break, brake   [1 mark]

Now try these

The children copy sentences, choosing the correct word to complete each sentence. Afterwards, ask the children to tell you the meanings of the words they didn't use. Together, make up sentences for the unused words 'brake', 'mail', 'scene', 'rains', 'reigns' and 'break'.

Answers

1. *Tariq was determined to break all his racing records.*   *[example]*

2. A male sheep is called a ram.   [1 mark]

3. It was the biggest cake I had ever seen.   [1 mark]

4. The reins were made of leather.   [1 mark]

5. To stop the car, press down on the brake.   [1 mark]

Support, embed & challenge

Support

Work with these children on recognising the different words: 'ball', 'bawl', 'male', 'mail', 'brake', 'break', 'rain', 'rein', 'reign', 'seen' and 'scene'. Recap the meaning of each word then place the word cards (see Additional resources) face down in a pile in the centre of the group. Ask the children to take turns to pick up a card and read it. Challenge the children to say what the word means, using the word in a sentence if they prefer. If they can say the meaning of the word, they get to keep the card.

Ask the children to complete Unit 25 Resource 1: Have you seen these spellings? (**Answers** ball – sphere for kicking or catching, bawl – cry loudly or shout, male – gender that is not female, mail – delivered letters or parcels, brake – mechanically slow down a vehicle, break – fall apart or stop working, rain – water droplets from clouds, rein – leather straps to control animals, reign – hold royal office, seen – see (in the past), scene – section of a play)

Embed

Organise the children into pairs and give each pair a set of word cards and definition cards (see Additional resources). This game works best if both sets of cards look identical when placed face down. Tell the children to use the cards to play a game of 'Pairs', pairing the words and their meanings.

Ask the children to complete Unit 25 Resource 2: Spellings to make or break you. (**Answers** 1. seen, 2. mail, 3. break, 4. mane, 5. scene, 6. rain, 7. ball, 8. brake)

Challenge

Ask these children to write three sentences, each using the word 'break' in a slightly different way, as in 'to break a record', 'to break a cup' and 'a short rest between chores'.

Homework / Additional activities

Spelling test

Ask the children to learn the following sentences.

We kicked the ball against the wall.	We went inside because of the rain. What a pain!
"It's not fair!" he bawled.	Charlie used the reins to rein in his horse.
Press the back of the scooter to brake.	Our queen has had a long reign.
Please break each egg.	Have you seen my green coat?
Male birds are more colourful that female birds.	Dad took photos of every scenic scene.
Can you mail my airmail letter?	

Collins Connect: Unit 25

Ask the children to complete Unit 25 (See Teach → Year 3 → Spelling → Unit 25).

Review unit 3

A. Ask children to look at each picture and write the word.

1. tongue [1 mark]

2. queue [1 mark]

3. scissors [1 mark]

4. muscles [1 mark]

5. eight [1 mark]

6. neighbour [1 mark]

B. Ask children to copy and complete the sentences with the correct apostrophes

1. The bunnies' ears were fluffy. [1 mark]

2. Both tables' legs were wobbly. [1 mark]

3. Tony's house is just down the road from mine. [1 mark]

4. The swimmers' teeth were chattering after their swim in the sea. [1 mark]

5. We stayed at the water's edge and paddled. [1 mark]

6. After two days' rest, the hikers were ready to start walking again. [1 mark]

C. Ask children to copy and complete the sentences with the missing words.

1. Guess who's coming to stay tomorrow! [1 mark]

2. Everyone except Josh can go and get their coats. [1 mark]

3. Medals were hung round the necks of the children who came first, second and third. [1 mark]

4. "Oh no! Not cabbage!" groaned Ruby and Cavan. [1 mark]

5. Sadly, my new boots rub and have given me a blister on my heel. [1 mark]

6. It was a foggy day and soon we were lost in the mist. [1 mark]

7. Can you meet me by the clock tower? [1 mark]

8. Come and see me after the lunch break and I will help you. [1 mark]

9. You must obey the safety rules at the adventure park. [1 mark]

10. We checked the weight of our bags before we left for the airport. [1 mark]

Begin at the beginning

Sort these words into the correct funnel.
Then add **–ing** and write them in the correct jars.

offer   signal   water   forget   travel   open   begin

The stress is on the first syllable and it doesn't end in **l**

The stress is on the second syllable or it ends in **l**

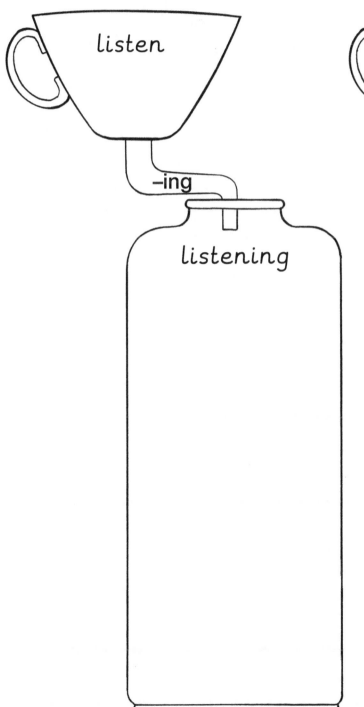

listen

label
upset

–ing

–ing

listening

labelling
upsetting

Marvell<u>ous</u> spell<u>ings</u>

Add the suffixes to the root words.

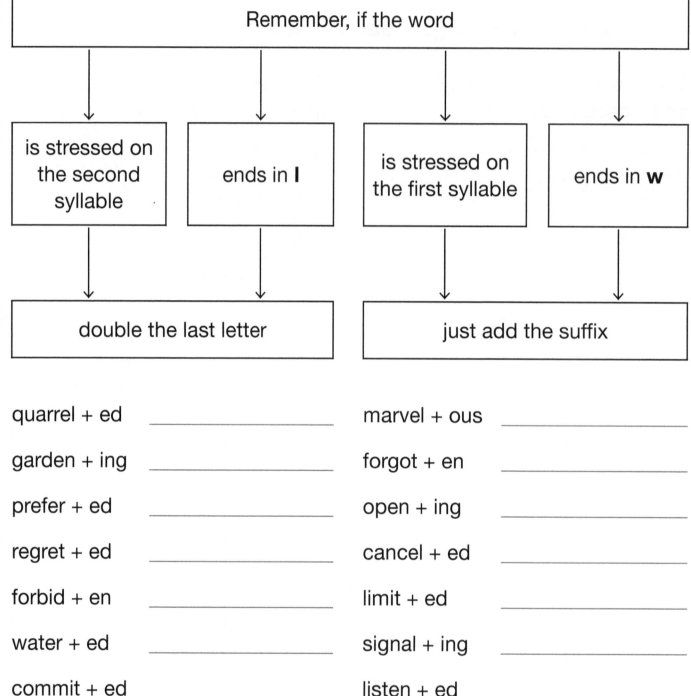

Remember, if the word			
is stressed on the second syllable	ends in **l**	is stressed on the first syllable	ends in **w**
double the last letter		just add the suffix	

quarrel + ed _____

garden + ing _____

prefer + ed _____

regret + ed _____

forbid + en _____

water + ed _____

commit + ed _____

travel + ing _____

occur + ing _____

marvel + ous _____

forgot + en _____

open + ing _____

cancel + ed _____

limit + ed _____

signal + ing _____

listen + ed _____

label + ing _____

flow + ed _____

 © HarperCollins*Publishers* 2017

The syrup story

Read the story. Circle all the words that spell the /i/ sound y.

"Can we have some pancakes please, Mum?" Finn asked. "Yes, I'll make them quickly before I go to the gym," said Mum, going to the cupboard. "Oh no! We've run out of syrup again. It's a mystery where it goes!" said Mum. "We had a new bottle last week. Please can you cycle to the shop and buy some more?"

It was a typical Spring day – cold and sunny. As Finn cycled past the park, the sun made crystal patterns on the lake. He cycled carefully through the one-way system and arrived at the shop in no time. There was a huge pyramid of chocolates at the front of the shop and Finn remembered the pancakes. He quickly found the syrup with the leaf symbol on it. He paid the lady then zoomed home on his bike.

© HarperCollins*Publishers* 2017

Spelling's no mystery

Choose the correct spelling for each word.
Cross out the incorrect spellings.

syrup	sirup		myx	mix
Egypt	Egipt		crystal	cristal
symbol	simbol		sytuation	situation
hydeous	hideous		pyramid	piramyd
dyscuss	discuss		mystery	mistery
typical	tipycal		lynx	linx
diffycult	difficult		cymbal	cimbol
bicycle	bycicle		abysmal	aismal

© HarperCollins*Publishers* 2017

A couple of troublesome letters

Choose a word from the box to complete each sentence.

couple	double	trouble	younger	touch	rough	cousins

1. The footpath was very _____ and bumpy.

2. Sam and George are in _____ for fighting in the playground.

3. At the seaside, we had a _____ scoop of ice cream.

4. Don't _____ the cakes: they are not for you!

5. I have a _____ sister called May.

6. Jamie has two _____ who live in London.

7. We are going camping in a _____ of weeks.

Tough words to spell

Choose **u** or **ou** to complete these words.

1. tr_____ble

2. cr_____mb

3. _____mbrella

4. d_____ble

5. _____pset

6. l_____mp

7. c_____ple

8. ch_____ck

9. y_____ng

10. s_____ng

11. c_____sin

12. p_____ddle

13. t_____ch

14. b_____g

15. r_____gh

16. dr_____mmer

17. t_____gh

© HarperCollins*Publishers* 2017

I <u>dis</u>like <u>mis</u>spelling

Add **dis–** to these words. Read the word.

agree _____

appear _____

cover _____

like _____

Add **mis–** to these words. Read the word.

spell _____

taken _____

place _____

behave _____

© HarperCollins*Publishers* 2017

Disspell or misspell?

Which of these words exist? Cross out the words that don't.

distaken	mistaken
dislike	mislike
disunderstand	misunderstand
dishonest	mishonest
disguided	misguided
disorder	misorder
disappear	misappear
distake	mistake
displease	misplease
disspell	misspell
disable	misable
dislaid	mislaid
disgrace	misgrace
dislead	mislead
disjudged	misjudged

 © HarperCollins*Publishers* 2017

Incredible spellings

Sort these words into the correct boxes.

incorrect	irregular	impatient
incredible	illogical	impossible
inactive	irrelevant	immature

in–

indecent

im–

imbalance

ir–

irresistible

il–

illegal

Illuminating spellings

Which of these words exist? Cross out the words that don't.

irregular	ilregular
imresponsible	irresponsible
impatient	ilpatient
incorrect	imcorrect
ilpossible	impossible
imadequate	inadequate
insane	irsane
inexpensive	ilexpensive
iractive	inactive
incompetent	imcompetent
imcredible	incredible
insufficient	irsufficient

 © HarperCollins*Publishers* 2017

<u>Re</u> and <u>inter</u> search

Find the words in the list that begin with the prefixes **inter–** or **re–**. Write them down.

intercity	ready	read	instant
red	review	intercom	reed
restore	internet	reckon	rethink
inkling	react	remake	insect
replace	repack	invest	rewind

_____   _____

_____   _____

_____   _____

_____   _____

_____   _____

_____   _____

_____   _____

Adding <u>re–</u> or <u>inter–</u>

Add **re–** or **inter–** to the words in the bubble.
Use the new words to complete the sentences.

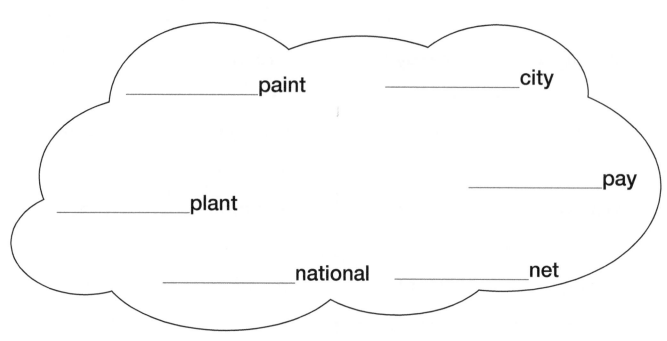

_____paint   _____city

_____pay

_____plant

_____national   _____net

1. The Nobel Prize is an _____ award.

2. We needed to _____ the walls after the tomato sauce explosion.

3. Mum had to _____ the bulbs after the dog had dug them up.

4. We took the _____ train from London to Birmingham.

5. Alfie cannot imagine life without the _____.

6. Rosie said I could _____ her when I had some pocket money.

                    © HarperCollins*Publishers* 2017

Superboy to the rescue!

Read this story. Circle all the words that start
with **super–** or **sub–**.

Superboy was walking through the subway on his way back
from the supermarket when his watch started bleeping.

"Danger at sea!" the message read. He dropped his shopping
and flew with supersonic speed to the coast.

Soon he was hovering over the ocean. His supersensitive
hearing told him there was a submarine in trouble below the waves.
He dived deeper and deeper into the water. The submarine was
submerged in a tangled mass of seaweed, trapped beneath fallen
rocks from an underwater avalanche. Summoning all his superhuman
strength, Superboy began to shift the rocks as fast as he could. But
Superboy was running out of air …

© HarperCollins*Publishers* 2017

Super jigsaw!

Cut out the tiles. Use them to create 15 words.
There should be no tiles left at the end.

super	super	super	super	super
super	sub	sub	sub	sub
sub	sub	sub	sub	sub
marine	hero	heading	size	title
star	merge	standard	vision	section
power	tract	way	store	scribe

© HarperCollinsPublishers 2017

Auto– or anti–: matching meanings

Write each word next to its meaning.

anticlockwise   antidote   antifreeze   autobiography

autograph   automatic   autopilot

1. _____ the opposite of the direction clock hands move in

2. _____ the written story of your own life

3. _____ your signature

4. _____ something that stops liquid freezing

5. _____ happens on its own

6. _____ cure for poison

7. _____ a device for steering an aircraft

© HarperCollinsPublishers 2017

The <u>anti</u>dote to spelling mistakes

Add **auto–** or **anti–** to these words. Write the new word by its meaning.

_____climax   _____clockwise   _____freeze   _____biography

_____graph   _____pilot   _____social_____mobile

_____bacterial   _____dote

---

1. _____   the opposite of the direction clock hands move in

2. _____   the written story of your own life

3. _____   a car

4. _____   your signature

5. _____   something that stops liquid freezing

6. _____   cure for poison

7. _____   a device for steering an aircraft

8. _____   behaviour that is bad for other people

9. _____   something that destroys bacteria

10. _____   a disappointing end to exciting events

    © HarperCollins*Publishers* 2017

Verb to noun transformations

Cut out the words. Match each root verb to its related noun.

Turn all the cards over, muddle them up and play a game of Pairs with a partner. A pair is a related verb and noun.

inform	observe	conversation	exploration
adore	determine	examination	inspiration
prepare	organise	organisation	preparation
inspire	examine	determination	adoration
explore	converse	observation	information

An explor<u>ation</u> of the suffix <u>–ation</u>

Add the suffix **–ation** to the verb in brackets at the end of each sentence. Use the new nouns to complete the sentences.

1. Rufus's _____ of Kitty's movements told him where she had hidden his teddy.   (observe)

2. We raised money for the _____ of the rainforest.   (conserve)

3. The X Factor is my _____ for becoming a singer.   (inspire)

4. _____ is everything when doing DIY.   (prepare)

5. Pushkal spent hours on the _____ of his Lego.   (organise)

6. The letter gave lots of _____ about the school trip.   (inform)

7. Everyone in Year 3 passed the _____ successfully.   (examine)

8. If there is any _____ of this noise, I will keep you in at break!   (continue)

© HarperCollins*Publishers* 2017

Hopefully using –ly easily

Add **–ly** to these words. Write the new words on the lines.
Remember, if the word ends in **–y** you must change it
to **i** before you add **–ly**.

shaky _____

ready _____

truthful _____

polite _____

uneasy _____

painful _____

local _____

tidy _____

Remove the **–ly** ending from these words. Write the new words on the
lines. Remember, you might need to turn an **i** back into a **y**.

endlessly _____

hopefully _____

funnily _____

greedily _____

crazily _____

dreamily _____

kindly _____

unkindly _____

© HarperCollins*Publishers* 2017

Spelling competent<u>ly</u> and confident<u>ly</u>

Add **–ly** to these words. Write the new words on the lines. Remember, sometimes you need to change the root word and sometimes you don't.

ordinary _____

beautiful _____

steady _____

childish _____

painful _____

horrible _____

entire _____

hopeless _____

hopeful _____

smart _____

healthy _____

large _____

feeble _____

wobble _____

close _____

lucky _____

speedy _____

definite _____

careful _____

 © HarperCollins*Publishers* 2017

Forbidden trea<u>sure</u>

Circle all the words in the story that have the **/zhur/** ending spelt **–sure.**

Jasmine heard the front door close. Her sister, Chloe, had gone out. Mum was at the leisure centre and Dad was busy outside making an enclosure for Jasmine's pet rabbit. Jasmine had been helping him measure the wood. But now she was free to sneak into her sister's room and enjoy the treasures hoarded in there.

First, she tried on all the jewellery. Then she experimented with the make-up. Jasmine giggled with pleasure. She didn't hear the front door open and close again or the footsteps up the stairs. Suddenly, Chloe was in the room, her displeasure written across her face in an angry scowl. The sudden exposure of the liberties she had taken made Jasmine flush bright red.

"This isn't how it looks," she mumbled, struggling to keep her composure.

"Really?" asked Chloe, narrowing her eyes. "Tell me how it is, then. I want a full disclosure."

Get the mea<u>sure</u> of spelling –<u>sure</u>

Cut out the words and use them to play a game of Pairs with a partner.

When you find a pair, your partner must keep the pair until you have correctly spelt the word.

closure	displeasure	leisure
composure	enclosure	measure
treasure	exposure	pleasure
closure	displeasure	leisure
composure	enclosure	measure
treasure	exposure	pleasure

© HarperCollins*Publishers* 2017

Sort it out: –ture, –cher or –tcher

Cut out the words and the three headings. Stick the headings at the top of a new piece of paper and stick each word under the correct heading.

/cher/ spelt –cher	/cher/ spelt –tcher	/cher/ spelt –ture
thatcher	nature	feature
archer	creature	
departure	scorcher	bencher
puncture	snatcher	
catcher	future	furniture
watcher	mixture	
adventure	voucher	pitcher
teacher	capture	
searcher	vulture	stretcher
picture	temperature	
moisture	butcher	richer
miniature	researcher	

© HarperCollins*Publishers* 2017

A spelling adven<u>ture</u>

Play this game with four players. You will need a set of word cards, a dice and a counter for each player.

- Take turns to roll the dice and move along the board.
- If you land on a WORD square, another player must draw a word card and read it to you. If you correctly spell the word, you may remain on your space. If you fail to spell the word, you must go back to your last square.
- The winner is the first to reach the FINISH square.

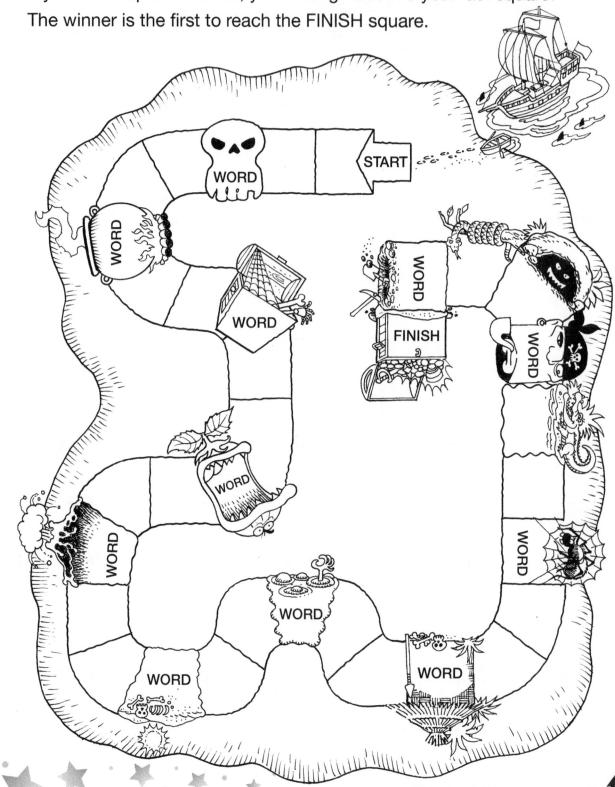

© HarperCollins*Publishers* 2017

A spelling explo<u>sion</u>!

Sort the words in the box into the correct star.

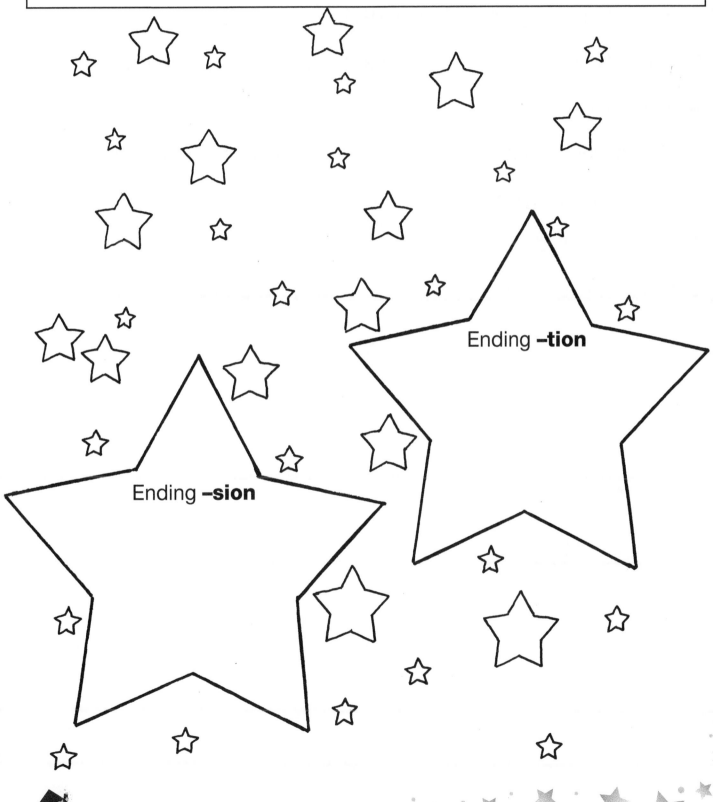

> vision   action   division   station   television   explosion   nation
> decision   confusion   condition   notion   information   occasion

Ending **–tion**

Ending **–sion**

© HarperCollins*Publishers* 2017

A difficult decision: –tion or –sion?

Choose **–tion** or **–sion** to complete the missing word. Remember, if the ending is the /zhun/ sound, then it will be spelt **–sion**.

1. The firework burst into an explo_____ of sparks.

2. Fish pie or cottage pie: it's your deci_____.

3. Your silly ac_____s have made me very embarrassed!

4. In all the confu_____, I forgot my coat.

5. Please read the informa_____ at the bottom of the page.

6. We sat in our pyjamas and watched televi_____.

7. The train pulled into the sta_____.

8. You are in no condi_____ to go to school.

 © HarperCollins*Publishers* 2017

Advantage<u>ous</u> –<u>ous</u> words

Add **–ous** to complete these words.

raven_____   nerv_____   obvi_____

ridicul_____   poison_____   hide_____

Use the words to complete the sentences.

1.   To be _____ is to be extremely silly.

2.   Deadly nightshade is so called because it is _____.

3.   The _____ system is a network of nerves found in animals.

4.   'Starving', 'famished' and '_____' all mean 'very hungry'.

5.   If something is _____, it is easy to see or understand.

6.   To be _____ is to be extremely ugly.

Spelling numer<u>ous</u> –<u>ous</u> words

Learn the words at the bottom of the page.

Underline the parts of the words that you find difficult.

Fold the words at the bottom of the page out of sight.

Write the adjectives related to each of these nouns.

ridicule _____

ambition _____

glory _____

hazard _____

poison _____

fury _____

disaster _____

glamour _____

nerve _____

danger _____

anxiety _____

suspicion _____

number _____

marvel _____

- -

**furious   marvellous   anxious   glorious   dangerous
hazardous   disastrous   ridiculous   suspicious   poisonous
ambitious   numerous   glamorous   nervous**

© HarperCollins*Publishers* 2017

Be a spelling magi<u>cian</u>

What jobs do these people do? Add the **–cian** ending and read each word.

1.

beauti_____

2.

electri_____

3.

magi_____

4.

musi_____

5.

techni_____

6.

mathemati_____

7.

politi_____

8.

opti_____

An educa<u>tion</u> in word exten<u>sion</u>

Match up each word in the box to the word from the same family.

Look at the spelling of each word. Is there anything to help you spell the longer word?

depression expression permission possession expansion
tension election eruption hesitation organisation
action direction information extension
option introduction education

possess _____   erupt _____

direct _____   act _____

depress _____   inform _____

express _____   expand _____

hesitate _____   organise _____

permit _____   opt _____

extend _____   introduce _____

tense _____   educate _____

elect _____

 © HarperCollins*Publishers* 2017

School bingo

Play this game with four players.

- Cut out the words and give two words to each player.

- Cut out the letters at the bottom of the page and put them in a bag.

- Ask someone to take out the letters one at a time and read them out.

- Cross off the letters in your word.

The winner is the first person to cross off all the letters in their words.

s c h o o l	c h o r u s	c h o i r	s c h e m e
e c h o	a n c h o r	c h a o s	a c h e

s	c	h	o	o	l	r	u	i	e	m	a	e

n

Improve your spelling technique

Read the words at the bottom of the page. Fold the words under, then use the words to complete the sentences.

1. An _____ is a device to stop ships from drifting.

2. It was total _____ at the children's party.

3. My friends and I sing in the school _____.

4. The shouts of the boys _____ around the tunnel.

5. I sit with my friends on the _____ bus every morning.

6. The loud music has given me a _____.

7. Jana ate all the strawberries and now her _____ hurts.

8. We all joined in singing the _____ after each verse.

- -

headache   chorus   chaos   choir

echoed   school   stomach   anchor

 © HarperCollins*Publishers* 2017

Be a spelling machine!

Look at these words. Colour all the words with the
/**sh**/ sound spelt **ch**.

chef	chimp	machete	wishes	quiche
shut	machine	cash	branch	which
slosh	wash	teach	sachet	charm
moustache	shopping	bashes	shipping	charade
chair	parachute	chalet	brochure	shrimp

© HarperCollins*Publishers* 2017

Lunch at the <u>ch</u>alet

Use the words in the box to fill in the gaps in the story.
Use each word once.

pistachios   machine   machete   chalet   parachuted
chef   quiche   brochures   sachet

Michelle could see the _____ from the plane.

She _____ down … and landed in a tree. She used

her _____ to free herself then entered the chalet. The

coffee _____ was bubbling away and her _____

had prepared her a delicious _____ for lunch, which she ate

with a _____ of mayonnaise. After lunch, she sat on the sofa

eating _____ and looking through holiday _____.

© HarperCollins*Publishers* 2017

A uni**que** challenge

Find a path across the dungeon.

Rules

Choose a square to start on.
/k/ spelt **k** = move down one square
/k/ spelt **c** = move up one square
/k/ spelt **que** = move right one square

Don't fall down any bottomless pits!

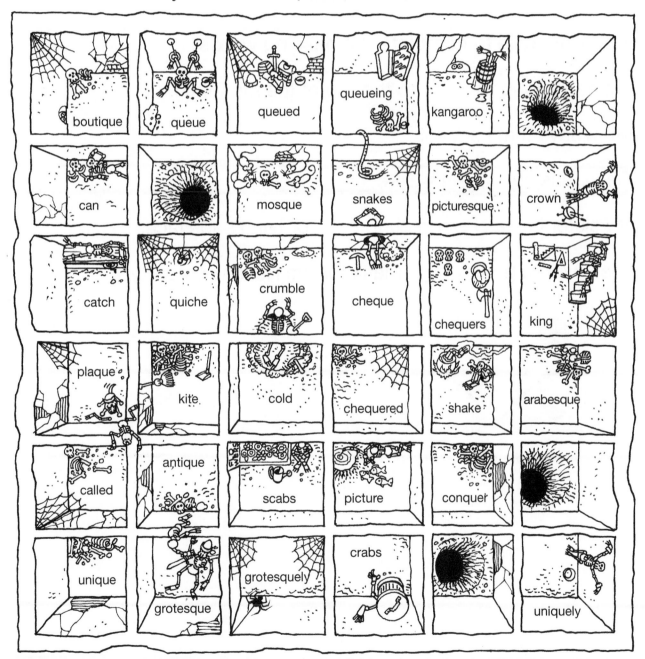

© HarperCollinsPublishers 2017

A catalogue of –que and –gue words

Choose **–g** or **–gue** to complete the missing words.

1. I bit my ton_____.

2. We went to see Ro_____ One at the cinema.

3. These socks don't belon_____ in the sitting room.

4. Manchester United are in the Premier Lea_____.

5. Finn and I looked at the Lego catalo_____.

Choose **–k** or **–que** to complete the missing words.

1. We had a long tre_____ to the top of the mountain.

2. Mum says that I am uni_____.

3. Georgia is my cousin's Gree_____ friend.

4. My sister has a clever techni_____ for tying shoe laces.

5. Ellen wore a grotes_____ mask for the Halloween party.

 © HarperCollins*Publishers* 2017

Searching for <u>sc</u>issors

Find these words in the word search.

| scene | scent | descend | crescent | science |
| scissors | muscles |

a	g	c	r	e	s	c	e	n	t	v
s	s	c	h	s	c	e	n	t	j	k
c	a	r	f	h	s	v	e	n	t	b
e	f	b	d	h	g	p	m	x	j	f
n	s	v	e	n	t	q	u	n	q	t
e	d	k	s	c	i	s	s	o	r	s
x	n	d	c	a	w	g	c	k	v	p
s	c	i	e	n	c	e	l	w	x	j
t	j	v	n	x	t	w	e	v	d	g
b	n	q	d	h	p	h	s	k	a	f
s	c	v	g	t	d	c	s	g	d	h

Spelling with <u>sc</u>

Read the words at the bottom of the page, then fold them out of sight.

Write each word under the correct picture.

1.

_____

2.

_____

3.

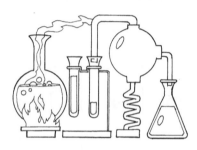

_____

4.

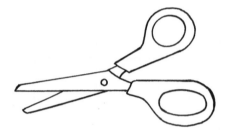

_____

5.

_____

6.

_____

7.

_____

- -

scissors   science   crescent   descend   scene   muscles   scent

© HarperCollins*Publishers* 2017

The aim of the game: Find words that sound the same

Look at the words. Find as many rhyming pairs as you can and write them at the bottom of the page. Remember, the spellings don't have to match for the words to rhyme.

prey   plate   tray

        veil   stale   train   delay

                                                    beige

    plane
                wait   sleigh   late
vein   great   crane

    rain
                                        obey
            pail
                        grey   fate
        ate
weight

                        eight   page   stage
            straight

    play   rate

_____ _____ _____ _____

_____ _____ _____ _____

_____ _____ _____ _____

_____ _____ _____ _____

_____ _____ _____ _____

_____ _____ _____ _____

_____ _____ _____ _____

_____ _____ _____ _____

© HarperCollins*Publishers* 2017

ei, eigh and ey crossword

Complete the crossword. All the answers contain the long /ay/ sound spelt **ei**, **ey** or **eigh**.

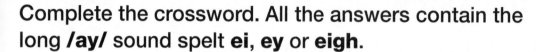

Across

1. a large sledge pulled by horses or reindeer

3. a colour between black and white

5. a tube that carries blood around your body

6. someone who lives next door

Down

2. the number 18

4. heaviness

7. the number 8

8. a pale brown colour

9. an animal that is hunted by a predator

© HarperCollins*Publishers* 2017

The nouns' apostrophes

Put the missing apostrophe in the correct place.

1.   The teachers pen is on her desk.

2.   The chairs leg is wobbly.

3.   Our dogs bark is very loud.

4.   My sisters best friend is Harriet.

5.   Todays book monitor is Alex.

Is the underlined word in each sentence singular or plural? Write the answer.

1. Next <u>month's</u> show will be Peter Pan. _____

2. All the <u>boys'</u> coats are on the floor. _____

3. The <u>tractor's</u> wheels are huge! _____

4. The <u>tractors'</u> wheels are huge! _____

5. Don't go too close to the <u>water's</u> edge. _____

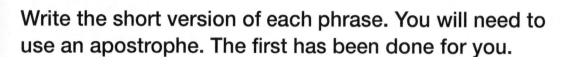

The apostrophes of the nouns

Write the short version of each phrase. You will need to use an apostrophe. The first has been done for you.

1. A holiday of one week   *One week's holiday*

2. A holiday of two weeks   _____

3. The hat of Sam   _____

4. The hats of the boys   _____

5. The light of the moon   _____

6. The light of the stars   _____

7. The work of the child   _____

8. The work of the children   _____

9. The eggs of the frog   _____

10. The eggs of the frogs   _____

11. The leaves of the tree   _____

12. The leaves of the trees   _____

© HarperCollins*Publishers* 2017

Who's accepting a spelling medal?

Draw a line to connect each word to its definition.

bury	not including
berry	the climate (rain, snow, sunshine)
accept	small juicy fruit
except	indication there is a choice
medal	metal disk on a ribbon
meddle	short for 'who is' or 'who has'
who's	interfere or fiddle
whose	put in a hole and cover
weather	belonging to whom
whether	agree to something

Effect versus affect

Read these definitions.

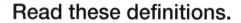

---

effect (noun): a result, as in cause and effect, or special effects

affect (verb): to influence

Write the missing word in each sentence. You can use the words more than once.

---

affect   affected   effect   effects

---

1.   The wind and rain badly _____ our game.

2.   We shook a metal sheet to give the _____ of a storm.

3.   Cry if you like, it won't _____ anything!

4.   Your high mark was the _____ of your hard work.

5.   The film had great special _____.

6.   It will _____ your mark if you don't use a capital letter.

© HarperCollins*Publishers* 2017

I've <u>heard</u> you're <u>great</u> at spelling!

Draw a line to connect each word to its definition.

hear	used to form a negative
here	this place
grate	shred or annoy
great	mend a wound
not	fastening of looped rope
knot	short for 'he will'
grown	big or wonderful
groan	emotional grunt
heel	back of the foot
heal	become bigger (in the past)
he'll	detect sound

© HarperCollins*Publishers* 2017

'Knot' not 'not'

Use the words in the box to complete the sentences.

hear   here   grate   great   not   knot   grown   groan
heel   heal   he'll

1.   Jonas says _____ come over after school.

2.   We can _____ raindrops tapping on the window.

3.   I always _____ when I'm told a bad joke.

4.   Come _____ now!

5.   Do _____ touch that!

6.   _____ the carrot and cabbage.

7.   We saw a _____ film on Friday.

8.   Millie has _____ her hair long.

9.   The scab on my knee is taking ages to _____.

10. My shoes rub my _____.

11. I can't undo the _____ in my shoe lace.

© HarperCollins*Publishers* 2017

Meet simple words with plain meanings

Draw a line to connect the word with its meaning.

Words	Meanings
meet	flesh for eating
meat	flying machine
mist	calm, quiet or stillness
missed	light fog
plain	obvious or basic
plane	come into the presence of
main	most important
mane	cost of a ticket to travel
piece	failed to catch or hit
peace	long hair on an animal's head
fare	part of something
fair	equal and just

TICKET 08644
ADMIT ONE
08644 ★★★

© HarperCollinsPublishers 2017

Spellings not to be <u>missed</u>

Use the words in the box to complete the sentences.
You will not need to use all the words.

mist	missed	mane	main	plane	plain	peace	piece
	meet	meat	fair	fare			

1. We will _____ Tamsin at the swimming pool at 2pm.

2. I was sad because I _____ Mummy.

3. We had to board the _____ very early in the morning.

4. The school office is by the _____ door.

5. Vegetarians do not eat _____.

6. I had _____ hair as a baby but now it's brown.

7. Go away and leave me in _____.

8. It's _____ to me that you have not washed!

© HarperCollins*Publishers* 2017

Have you <u>seen</u> these spellings?

Draw a line to match the word to its meaning.

ball
bawl
male
mail
brake
break
rain
rein
reign
seen
scene

fall apart or stop working
see (in the past)
cry loudly or shout
mechanically slow down a vehicle
sphere for kicking or catching
delivered letters or parcels
water droplets from clouds
hold royal office
gender that is not female
leather straps to control animals
section of a play

Spellings to make or <u>break</u> you

Use the words in the box to complete the sentences.
You won't need to use all the words.

ball   bawl   male   mail   brake   break   main mane rain rein reign seen scene

1. Have you _____ the snow outside?

2. I opened the _____ that arrived this morning.

3. We practised for half an hour then had a _____.

4. A male lion has a huge shaggy _____.

5. The burglar left a clue at the _____ of the crime.

6. The _____ fell from the clouds and soaked the ground.

7. We like to kick a _____ around the garden.

8. Ben found it hard to use the back _____ on his bike.

© HarperCollins*Publishers* 2017